T0339446

Team Unity

Based on more than ten years of researching, observing, coaching and building extraordinary teams, this entertaining and thought-provoking book demonstrates how to unify groups of all sizes to maximize performance.

Unity is the most influential factor in team performance, and although it is frequently discussed, it is often misunderstood. This book explains how disunity is the root cause of all team dysfunctions and provides clear instructions on how to define, measure and increase unity in your organization. Through entertaining and impactful stories, John Ross divides *Team Unity* into four components—focus, direction, trust and conflict—and examines how they are related and measured. Notably, Ross introduces *The Unity Formula*, a simple equation useful for leaders at all levels in any organization to measure the team's current unity and identify areas for improvement.

Senior and middle managers in manufacturing, hospitality, and a range of other industries, as well as entry level employees and students of organizational behavior and HRM, will find this book an invaluable resource for understanding how to identify, measure and partake in the right steps to increase team performance.

John Ross started his career as a seventh grade history teacher in Mesa, Arizona. From there he worked as a producer of musical events and then as a project lead at one of the world's leading manufacturers before becoming a business professor at Indiana University's southeast campus. He has been researching and working with teams for more than a decade. His research in extraordinary teams and unity has since expanded into hope, knowledge acquisition and retention. He holds a BA in organizational studies from Arizona State University, an MBA in finance from Drexel University and a PhD in management from New Mexico State University.

Team Unity

A Leader's Guide to Unlocking Extraordinary Potential

John Ross

Routledge
Taylor & Francis Group

NEW YORK AND LONDON

Cover image: Ivcandy (Getty images)

First published 2022
by Routledge
605 Third Avenue, New York, NY 10158

and by Routledge
4 Park Square, Milton Park, Abingdon, Oxon, OX14 4RN

Routledge is an imprint of the Taylor & Francis Group, an informa business

Library of Congress Cataloging-in-Publication Data
A catalog record for this title has been requested

ISBN: 9781032215808 (hbk)
ISBN: 9781032215778 (pbk)
ISBN: 9781003269038 (ebk)

DOI: 10.4324/9781003269038

Typeset in Sabon
by Apex CoVantage, LLC

To my best friend and four wonderful boys who are tired of Dad's daily discussions of unity.

Contents

Preface

People fascinate me, especially when they work together. Even before I officially began researching teams, I observed them around me—at school, at work, in sports. I even loved hearing about families, the original team unit. I admired extremely successful teams and investigated poor performing teams. I loved hearing about what made teams tick and marveled at how much more a group of people, unified in heart and mind, could accomplish than individuals striving alone.

My work adventures allowed me a view into diverse teams—in music, nonprofits, education, sports, healthcare, retail and manufacturing. I noticed that truly great, game-changing teams were extremely rare. Most teams were average; a fair share were terrible.

My interest fell with *extraordinary teams (ETs)*. I wanted to know what made them unique—and why they performed above the rest. In this pursuit, I developed my first official research question: *Of all the teams in the workplace, how were these "extraordinary" teams—with similar resources, time and people—able to accomplish so much more?*

I went to work on this project—interviewing team members, college students, professors and colleagues. I took their answers and compared them with the content in the large number of books and articles I was reading. Yet I didn't think any of the articles or books were getting to the source of team performance.

A few years later, a fellow researcher suggested I read the book *Hot Groups* about extremely high-performing teams, which she thought were similar to the ETs I was describing. Authors John Leavitt and Jean Lipman-Blumen described amazing teams that "felt like magic" or "felt like family," where the members didn't just work together, but they also played together. They truly cared about each other and ultimately about the success of their teams. Their accomplishments always exceeded expectations and led to incredible feats of creativity and ingenuity. *Finally! The these were the teams I was looking for!*

I pored through the book—highlighting, underlining, writing notes in the margins. Everything I read matched what I had discovered. The teamwork, the magic, the comradery, the love of the challenge, the sacrifice, the fun! I loved every minute of reading the book . . . until the end.

After describing these amazing teams—complete with stories of Navy Seals, pilots, athletes, surgeons and so many others—John and Jean dropped the bomb: *They didn't know how these groups had formed!* They knew certain environmental conditions were necessary, but beyond that, they offered no ingredients or formula for creating a high-performing, unified team. On the contrary, they called them "random." They said that all a person could do was create the conditions for a hot group—and *hope* that it formed.

This sparked my research fury. Within hours, I had opened team textbooks and articles, looking for a more complete explanation. A textbook confirmed the authors' premise, stating that while those rare ETs were great, amazing and wonderful, they were random at best.

I began to realize I wouldn't find what I sought within existing research about these exemplary teams. That is because no one knew how to form them. The process of my discovery—and what it meant to my research and ultimate premise—is discussed further in the book.

The impact of this discovery cannot be understated. I knew at that moment my path had been set. Challenge accepted. For the next several years, I read and researched teams of all kinds but mostly the extraordinarily performing teams. I found them almost everywhere and was fortunate to interview and study members of such teams.

After my findings began to coalesce around a common structure, I called Jean Lipman-Blumen to discuss her findings and share my own. We had a wonderful conversation that lasted well over an hour. When I shared my findings, she was overjoyed to hear that I had continued her research. It is with her blessing that I continue what she and John started almost 25 years ago. As I describe later, the meeting with Jean was a momentous occasion for me. I still remember exactly where I was when we spoke and can still hear the joy and passion in her voice, talking about one of her favorite subjects nearly 20 years after the publication of her book.

Despite knowing that I had a new premise on teams which could benefit many leaders, managers and even professors like myself, I hesitated when writing this book. I knew I couldn't make it "just another teams book." There are already plenty of books on teams. I wanted my book to have more direct application to the front-line leaders, not just academics. I wanted to provide a mix of theory and application. Therefore, besides exploring the four key components of team unity, I share The Unity Formula—a formula I created for evaluating team unity, along with some of my findings while using the formula with well over 100 teams—ranging from executives to interns in the manufacturing, education, athletics, healthcare, retail, hospitality and entertainment industries.

I designed The Unity Formula as a tool to help measure how much of a team's full potential is realized in their current operating conditions—and then provide a path with key areas to direct attention to improve a team.

Sometimes we overcomplicate teamwork. The Unity Formula simplifies the analysis of a team's potential, so it can be used by any interested party—not just by high-paid consultants.

As proof that The Unity Formula works beyond the classroom or as another interesting theory, the model has been extremely well-received by those actually using it in the workplace. It is for that reason that I look forward to sharing it with you all.

It is in both my opinion and experience that the precepts of this book can heal families, empower social movements and invigorate organizations. Unity is the number one contributor to team performance. Whatever team, large or small, you may find yourself, if you choose to invest your time to increase unity, you will see tremendous results.

Besides learning key principles to improve your teams, I hope you enjoy the book. I hand selected unique stories from a wide variety of industries and time periods to help illustrate the points described in the book. It has taken me over a decade to feel comfortable enough with the research to write a book. I've engaged in a vast amount of work to uncover what makes an ET, but I tremendously enjoyed the journey. I've aimed to make this book accessible—and enjoyable—for you, too.

John Ross

Introduction

I'd like to start this book with an activity.

Think of the best team you've ever been on—the *absolute* best. It could have been a group of friends, family, sports team, work team or collection of people in any circumstance who came together to accomplish a goal. Once you have the team in your mind, I'd like you to write what made it great. Think about details around the emotions and behaviors of the leader and team members. What do you think made that team great? Write it here:

_____

_____

_____

_____

Now, think of the worst team you've ever been on—the *absolute* worst. The team where your stomach dropped just thinking about having to work with them. What made that team horrible? Write those emotions, leader behaviors, team member behaviors, etc., here:

_____

_____

_____

_____

Hopefully, you were able to think of a good team. Some have difficulty finding such an example, which is terrible to think about!

Now let's explore your findings. From the interviews and research I've conducted with others who were asked these questions, I'll surmise that some of the traits of the best team you've ever been on may include *family, magic, awesome, fun, motivating* and *hard-working*, to name a few.

What about the worst team you've ever been on? I have yet to meet a person that has difficulty thinking of a terrible team experience. Often

DOI: 10.4324/9781003269038-1

people struggle less with deciding whether they've had a negative example but rather can't decide which negative team example to choose. Here you might have written things like *terrible, no one worked, boss was never there, didn't know what we were doing, boss yelled at us* and maybe even something about a *lack of respect.*

I used to start every class I taught going through this exercise, except I'd ask participants to tell me about the best and worst classes they had been in. As a business professor and workplace consultant, I've learned some parallels between the classroom and workplace—especially in that they both involve people and can be greatly influenced by how those people engage with one another. The classroom, as with many groups in life, is a team. The student's job is to learn. Mine is to teach. When we work together, we have a great experience. This exercise helps set the groundwork for establishing unity in the classroom. It encourages student engagement, as students enjoy talking about their best class experiences. And when it comes to sharing detailed information about their worst class experiences, they absolutely do not shy away.

Once we have our list created, we talk about the items on it and create an agreement: *I agree to do my best to mimic the best class ever and avoid doing things that create a negative learning environment, if they agree to do the same.* I enjoy this activity. It sets the tone of the class, creates a discussion everyone can participate in and gets us all on the same page. We want this class to be awesome. In order to do that, the students and the professor must work together.

That's true of this book as well.

You and I must work together. I want all of your current and future teams to be excellent, and if they're not excellent, I want to equip you to figure out where they need improvement. I want you to enjoy being on a team because being a member of an extraordinary team (ET) is so rewarding that it is an absolute shame more people don't experience its benefits more often. This book will help you learn how to craft agreements with your team to strive for the right things—those that will matter to your team performance and unity.

Many studies have been conducted on team performance, as I hinted at in the preface. One of the most interesting is a group out of MIT that used small recording devices to record interactions between team members.[1] They used the devices on thousands of teams in a wide variety of situations and industries. They discovered that the higher the performance of the team, the more interactions they engaged in. Then they discovered that the quality of their performance wasn't just influenced by the *frequency* of their interactions, but the *quality* of those interactions mattered as well. Their unique and innovative study, along with their findings, have been discussed in numerous articles and books. Ultimately, they narrowed team success down to five key traits. Their premise states that the more a team instills the following five traits into their practices, the more successful they'll be:

1. Everyone on the team talks and listens in roughly equal measure, keeping contributions short and sweet.
2. Members face one another, and their conversations and gestures are energetic.
3. Members connect directly with one another—not just with the team leader.
4. Members carry on back-channel or side conversations within the team.
5. Members periodically break, go exploring outside the team, and bring information back.[2]

These are useful principles and definitely applicable to teamwork settings, but this information, while excellent and highly recommended, does not explain *why* the behaviors exist in high-performing teams nor would these actions necessarily lead to a better team. These are the actions that great teams have in common, but the study does not conclude *how* and *why* these actions came to exist among these great teams.

- *To ensure time was spent together, did these great teams assign a timekeeper to manage the amount of time each person spoke?*
- *To ensure the team members communicated, did these teams assign a communications intern to keep track of interactions and send emails when side conversations were too low?*
- *Was there a reward and punishment system to ensure these five traits remained in place throughout the project?*

The answer to these is an obvious no. The five suggestions above from the MIT study happened naturally. No one monitored their behavior to ensure that they happened. In other words, the five suggestions are not prescriptive. Just because you force these five traits to exist doesn't mean your team will be great. Rather than being the contributing elements of a great team, these actions are consequences or evidence of a great team. These are actions that great teams participate in, but it is not the cause of the great team. The question I sought to answer, then, was *how did they get to excellence, where all of these symptoms of high-performing teams were observable?*

When I decided to study high-performing teams to determine how they came about, I found that while they all had their unique behaviors, cultures and practices—many of which have been written in books—they all had something else in common. They were all *unified.*

What does it mean to be unified? It means that no matter the team, the project, the industry, the time period, the circumstance or the context, the common factor behind every ET is *an extreme connection in desires for accomplishment*. They were of *one heart and one mind*. They were *united in team goals and committed to a strategy. They were free of judgement and discord. After years of research, I've discovered that there are four main components to unity*. We will explore the concept of unity more as we delve into the four components of unity in future chapters.

At this point in my research, I felt the need to expound on unity—what it looks like, feels like, sounds like and most important how to increase it. We know it when we see it, although no one has adequately defined what comprises it. We know when a team is not unified, although we don't know with any specific measurement tool what put them into such a state.

My hope, based on my research, is that this book explains the process behind achieving unity—and thereby helps you increase your team's positive interactions and performance. Not only will unity be observable in your team—but measurable as well. Even better, by increasing unity as outlined in this book, their performance should be repeatable—both within the same team and within any future teams you may manage.

While we think of teams as those in the workplace, this book will help you recognize levels of unity in any group that you may find yourself within, including families, social gatherings, volunteer organizations, religious groups, etc. Suggestions on how to increase unity are provided, along with a quick and easy diagnostic tool.

Being on a team, whether formal or informal, can be an extremely rewarding experience. I hope this book helps increase the rewards in your life.

This book is meant to be hands on. It starts with setup information that is crucial to understanding teams (Part 1: Introducing Unity). Then it explores a description of the four key elements of unity (Part 2: Defining Unity). Finally, The Unity Formula is introduced in Part 3 (Measuring Unity) and explained—with areas provided for you to practice using it. Then in Part 4 (The Unity Formula), additional suggestions for improvement are offered for each of the four key components presented.

Notes

1. Pentland, A. S., Wooley, A., & Malone, T. W. (2015, July 15). The new science of building great teams. *Harvard Business Review*, Harvard Business Publishing. hbr.org/2012/04/the-new-science-of-building-great-teams
2. Pentland, A. S., Wooley, A., & Malone, T. W. (2015, July 15). The new science of building great teams. *Harvard Business Review*, Harvard Business Publishing. hbr.org/2012/04/the-new-science-of-building-great-teams

Part 1

Introducing Unity

Chapter 1

What Makes an Extraordinary Team?

We are all, to some degree, *people people*. We are motivated by positive connections in our lives and demotivated when that supply of appreciation, affirmation and human connection is cut off.[1]

Isolation punishment is so powerful that it is often used as a deterrent in prisons. It's also used as a tool in interrogation tactics because people are willing to sacrifice loyalty and divulge information in exchange for the promise to protect or reconnect with a loved one or close contact.

Parents use this concept to their advantage. When applying punishment, the isolation may come in the form of a time-out. On the contrary, when a child is rewarded, they are often allowed to see their friends. As a parent, you may say something like, "If you clean your room, then you can go to the pool with your friends" or "If you help me make dinner, then you can take the car to the movie with Alex."

When adults achieve something at work, the celebration likewise often includes other people. You may have a team pizza party for a job completed or all go out after work to rejoice in successfully meeting a milestone.

While we could celebrate on our own or live in isolation for a time, we crave the elements that come from being part of a group. In some way or another, we need interaction with people.[2]

Not only do we need people, but we also need to be accepted by them.[3]

Some might say, "Not me" or "I prefer to be alone." Many people prefer and may even seek moments of solitude. Being alone definitely can be relaxing. If you think about some of the biggest stresses in your life, other people probably caused at least some of them. It isn't bad to want to be alone to shut out such stress.

After a while, though, just about everyone seeks acceptance from others. In fact, Boston Consulting Group conducted a study of more than 200,000 people in 2014, and of ten key factors, participants rated "appreciation" for their work the most important to their engagement and happiness within the workplace. Number two was "good relationships with colleagues." These ranked well above such factors as job security, salary and even relationship with one's boss.[4]

DOI: 10.4324/9781003269038-3

The connection that people seek could be achieved in person or online groups; either way, it is key to wellness and ultimately performance. In fact, recent research shows that *inclusion therapy*, the act of helping to develop a person's belief that they are not alone and that there are others around them that love them and support them, has been extremely potent in the improvement of depression and anxiety.[5]

In short, we can conclude from this research that people are awesome. We seek company for comfort, love, entertainment, support and accomplishment.

Teams Are Personal

I've shared how my research came about, but I'd like to back up a bit, so you understand what drives me as your author. The truth is, I love people. I'm fascinated by them. I love hearing their stories, their interests, their beliefs—the who, what, why and how of a person's life.

I also love when people come together, especially at work. And I've always been fascinated by *how* people work together—even before I began researching team success.

My first job was at a movie theater. It was a minimum wage job at an eight-screen theater in Texas, situated on the border of four high school districts. Every night, weekend and holiday, 60 of us would work at the theater, serving hundreds of customers. We had a tremendous time. Several customers drove from many miles away because of our service. It wasn't necessarily the management; the secret was we truly loved what we did. We loved being together. I enjoyed making customers laugh and providing the freshest popcorn around. I have so many ridiculous stories from those two and a half years. At the time, I just knew I loved going to work, but I now recognize how unique it was for a large group of teenagers to enjoy working together for so long. We had a very low turnover rate. There were definitely times when the job didn't get done as well as it should have, but we were passionate about what we did. One could say that we were *unified*.

Several of us are still in touch. Our children have met. One person in the group became a major celebrity. We all celebrated her success. Two former coworkers married each other. Our team was extremely tight.

How tight, you ask? The movie theater eventually sold and was being torn down. The theater experience meant so much to us that someone had a great idea to hold a reunion there. Many of our team showed up. Our old managers showed up. It was a great time. And it wasn't because of the building we worked in—but the people we worked with and what we accomplished together.

Seeing how much work had brought us together sparked my interest in teams. *Why couldn't more teams be like that?* I wondered.

As we grew up, life started getting in the way. Money didn't matter much when we worked at the movie theater. We all lived at home with very few bills. As people grow up, they acquire grown-up issues. Money, children, partners, spouses, bosses, school, promotions, respect, status, family, economy, government and more start invading thoughts. Everyone in the workplace stresses over something. In today's hyperconnected world, home problems follow us to work, and work problems follow us home. A boss can get in touch with us while we are waiting at a red light or a baseball game. Our family can reach us during a meeting or while working on a project. We can check our bank accounts on our phones. Anywhere our smartphones are, the rest of our lives follow. And with many working virtually, the lines become even more blurry. We had a great time at the theater and worked on great projects, but we had all gone our separate ways and life took over.

As I took on other roles, it appeared as if the great days of teamwork at the movie theater were over. It was time to grow up and start "adulting," a term we millennials use to refer to the process of becoming less fun and more stressed. I needed to accept that this was how life must be from here on out—if I were to be *successful*.

This is common to how many of my students feel today. They're timid about graduating because they have to grow up and get "bills," and I don't mean dollar bills. I've met many adults who still feel the same way that I felt as a young man after high school: *Teams are going to be lame from here on out.*

Then I returned to the seventh grade. Not like Adam Sandler in *Billy Madison*. As a teacher.

Many people would not associate working with 12- and 13-year-olds as a defining moment of leadership and teamwork. In fact, many would consider my years as a teacher as training in survival skills. No doubt, teaching junior high can be tough, but I absolutely loved my years with my students.

I started off as a seventh-grade history and English teacher at a small junior high in a very low socioeconomic area of Arizona. I was making $24,000 a year. For the record, at the time of writing this, I am not a very old man reflecting back on days when hamburgers were a nickel. $24,000 was very low even for that time. To give you an idea, my school offered insurance, but informally, I was told just to apply for state benefits because I made so little that I'd easily qualify. As a comparison, many fast-food places today pay $15 an hour starting wage, or over $30,000 a year working full time.

My wife taught dance part time while raising our children. We had a small house, two cars and a large stack of bills. Money was a stressful topic. I worried every night about covering my mortgage and utilities. It was definitely a crazy period in my life that I probably didn't handle too well at times, but fate had put me in that place to show me a very important lesson.

I learned that despite circumstances, teams can still be awesome. I had a group of seventh graders with all sorts of issues common in low socio-economic areas with drugs and abuse. I was even told that these students, as sixth graders, had tested the lowest that the school had ever tested, but we still had an amazing time.

The students excelled at anything I gave them. Granted, most of what I gave them in the first few weeks was remedial work from the fourth grade. Many of my students had been uprooted many times. Each time a child moved during the school year, gaps would form in their education. One of my students had moved 24 times in two years. In seventh grade, she struggled with the mere definitions between city, state and country. Most students in my class were below grade level and poor constructors of sentences. I started where they were, and they grew quickly.

As they grew, I found myself setting aside my numerous life issues and focusing on this positive and wonderful thing that was happening in my classroom. The more the class improved, the less outside stress bothered me. I became more hopeful that we'd be able to overcome whatever challenges our little class may experience.

The students felt the same way. Many of my 12- and 13-year-olds had experienced more hardships in life than I had ever experienced, even though I also came from blue-collar parents. They struggled with many learning disadvantages and home stresses, but when we were together, things were different. They left all of that behind. They were themselves in our room, and were experiencing great success in the classroom, some for the first time ever. Because their school life was improved, the students were able to handle their home lives a little easier.

Some of the parents, many of whom were working multiple jobs, began volunteering with classroom activities—the first time ever for some. Our amazing team not only impacted our lives but those around us as well.

There were many other signs of success in this class. Word spread of our class's success. Enrollment in our tiny school was busting at the seams. Parents were withdrawing children from other schools just to attend my seventh-grade class. By the end of the year, the students in my class were in the 90th percentile in the nation for reading in year one and 85th percentile in the nation for year two. Our grade raised more money than any other grade in a Mesa/Phoenix-wide charity competition, an impressive feat being the lowest income school in the competition; our class donated more cans for the canned food drive than any other class in the school. We killed it at everything we did. We event printed T-shirts with our successes, which I still have today.

Fast forward several years. I had been a part of several other teams but none that I would call extraordinary. There were definitely some great ones but none that reached the same level as we had in my classroom. As

I reflected on why this classroom had been so special, it seemed that fates had to align just right for an extraordinary team (ET) to happen, almost as if ETs were random.

This belief was reinforced by several books, which suggested you could no sooner predict an ET than you could predict where a tornado would land or where the next lighting strike would happen. These super high-performing teams were random and thus thrown out of team research. As outliers, they seemed impossible to study—and perhaps more important, irrelevant, since there would be nothing anyone could do to influence their creation.

Then, as a project lead in a major manufacturing company, I heard of another team that was accomplishing some extraordinary things.

My job position provided me the opportunity to travel throughout the entire plant. I heard several executives talking about how this new director got lucky—that everything had been set up for him, that he had the most resources and the best people—so of course he was successful. I knew that wasn't true because I had known the area he took over before he arrived. It was a forgotten area, an area where no one wanted to be, because it was so unsuccessful that many felt it a career-damaging move. But this person had turned it around.

I also knew he hadn't been provided many, if any, extra resources, because I remembered when he was hired. He was new to aerospace. His hiring was in question from the start. What could he possibly show us aerospace professionals at one of the world's largest companies? After his success in his new position, they challenged his luck again with a different position, new challenges and additional responsibilities on top of his new position. He achieved tremendous results again. It almost seemed easy for him.

Clearly, this guy knew something about how to create an ET. He had a track record, with several examples of leading ETs. He wasn't following a script, but he knew intuitively how to inspire a team to perform at very high levels. While he hadn't yet defined his steps, he knew how to recreate success within a team. That's why his resume impressed the vice presidents when he was hired, and that's why he continued to have success. I was convinced it was not luck. It was not extra resources. It was not having the most skilled people on his team. He was successful in two consecutive attempts, in spite of any roadblocks.

Extraordinary Teams Are Not Random—or Static

It was then that it hit me. Contrary to many books, *ETs are not random!* ETs cannot be random. If they were random, then what about the true stories of teachers who did tremendous things with groups of people, as documented in several movies—such as Erin Gruwell in *Freedom*

Writers, Francois Begaudeau in *The Class*, Jaime Escalante in *Stand and Deliver* and Joe Clark in *Lean on Me*? These teachers weren't just one-hit wonders. They delivered tremendous results year after year. They must have had an idea of how building an ET was accomplished.

What about coaches? Why are millions of dollars spent on college football coaches, unless the athletic department is confident they know how to build a team? Coach Phil Jackson of the Bulls moved to the Lakers in 1999 and won three more championships, then two more a few years later. Many have said that he had the talent with Kobe Bryant and Shaquille O'Neil, so of course he won, but Kurt Rambis and Del Harris also had amazing talent on the team before Phil arrived, yet it was Phil who led the Lakers to five championships. Several of the biggest stars in the NBA have played on the Phoenix Suns, but the Suns haven't won a championship. Luke Walton had tremendous talent with the Lakers—including one of the all-time greats, Lebron James—but the team still had some of the worst records of the century under his leadership.

I realize sports are a sensitive subject for some and that there are a million other variables that contribute to a winning team than just a coach—but there's definitely something key about a coach who knows how to develop a winning team.

Also, the ETs that I researched and worked with seemed to grow from normal teams. The teams I read about were not already *almost extraordinary* and then just suddenly became great. Many of these teams came from average or below average and became great.

As I grew in my career, as I worked with supervisors, team leads and managers, a common belief upheld by many was that their team was either *good or not*, as if it were a binary distinction. Many in leadership positions believed their teams were hopeless or filled with such trouble-making people that they would be successful as managers just by preventing a fight. Many would say, "Well, this isn't a good crew, but I used to have a great crew. . . ." I couldn't believe people were telling me this! And this defeatist rhetoric didn't just come from the manufacturing organization I worked for, which was a Fortune 100 company that hired from some of America's top universities. I received the same responses as I interviewed people from many different industries. I heard it time and time again.

Labeling a team as inferior is not productive. Not only does it provide an excuse for the leader not to try, but the leader sets the tone. If the leader isn't trying, then the team members will be less likely to try as well.

When people say their team is no good, really what they're saying is, "I'm not exactly sure what to do with this team" like fishermen who say, "Well, they're just not biting today. . . ."

I used to work with a professional fisherman. He called himself the "Fishing Ninja" because when he was in tournament mode, he moved across his boat in lightning speeds, checking all of his lines. I asked him once if he believed the phrase "the fish just weren't biting today." He was shaking his head before I finished the question. "Absolutely not. It doesn't matter what day it is, the time of day, the weather or water conditions—fish need to eat. You have to match the right lure and use it correctly to catch the fish. Fish are always biting when I go out."

There's another story of an 80-plus-year-old Italian woman who used to teach my Sunday School class when I was 12 years old. She taught energetically and passionately. She always wore her crocheted yarn shawl and didn't move very quickly, but we loved hearing her stories. She was born in the early 1900s and had lived through The Great Depression, World War II, The Korean War, The Vietnam War, The Cold War, a presidential assassination, The Civil Rights movement, 1970s music (with a few exceptions) and all sorts of other calamities—but she was such a positive person. To every class, at least once, she'd say, "There are no such things as bad people, just people making bad choices."

Being smart 12-year-olds, we would throw out world dictators to see what she would say. "What about Hitler?" "What about Stalin?"

Her reply? "Well, they made a lot of bad choices."

It wasn't until I got older that I really understood what she was saying. People who make poor choices still have *hope*. They can turn things around and make good choices. They may not choose to make good choices—or they may face circumstances that challenge them to even see their options—but options are always there. It was true for Darth Vader when he saved his son's life; it must be true for everyone else.

Let's combine the lessons from these two stories into teams. What if teams weren't "biting" or performing because they had inexperienced leaders? Maybe if the right leader were put into place, someone who would correctly use the right lures at the right time, then the team would always be performing. Maybe there was no such thing as a bad team but rather just a team making poor choices—but if the team were given the right opportunity and if inspired enough, maybe they would make good choices. That would be a big deal, right? Just starting with that mindset could make a huge difference.

This is what I mean about greatness—and success—not being binary. You don't either have it or not. Despite any lack of success, you always have the opportunity to take steps toward it.

The same applies to teams. Despite how down in the dumps your team may seem, its performance can improve. Increasing unity can help you increase your performance even if you never make it to an extraordinary level. Every team has a chance to be a good team.

I found evidence to support this idea that team success can improve, based on hope and belief in that improvement. The people I interviewed who had built one or more ETs always seemed to lead teams that performed at high or extraordinary levels. They *loved* their teams and spent as much time as possible with them. It's almost as if they looked at their teams as a puzzle, trying to figure out the right combination to maximize success. They would frequently express their desires to ditch their required paperwork because they'd rather be with their teams. They seemed to readily share new stories about approaches they were trying with their teams or milestones they had achieved. They were smiling. Their teams had been part of a success story—making their careers entertaining and their work enjoyable.

Why Push for an Extraordinary Team?

It makes sense why these team leaders would invest time in their teams. Their teams experienced success because these leaders chose to *invest* their time into their teams. The success of their teams increased each leader's status in the organization. If their teams achieved goals, then both the leaders and the team members received good reviews at the end of the year—which led to pay raises and opportunities for upward mobility.

For leaders, teams are not an incidental tool but rather a source of career success. For extraordinary leaders, teams are their hobbies, their research interests, their passions.

Those who had never led a high- or extraordinary-performing team tended to continue producing low to average team results. For them, their teams were a source of stress. They were not happy discussing their teams. The discussion frequently led to singling out individual members and discussing the problems that they had caused. They seemed exhausted. They appeared to look forward to meetings with their colleagues away from their teams and were reluctant to return to their teams. They talked about themselves a lot as well—versus focusing on the well-being or achievements of those on their teams.

I learned that many of the executives and managers that I've worked with over the years had never had or been a part of an ET. They accepted the excuses discussed earlier—that there were just *bad teams, bad timing, bad issues,* etc. Nothing to be done. But fortunately, the low to average team leaders were "saved" from disastrous teams and moved to new areas (sarcasm intended).

Average team performance was the norm. The ET leaders were the weird ones, the outliers.

At this point, you might be thinking, "Why try? Why try if both types of team leaders are probably going to be promoted the same anyway? Why put forth the effort and energy into creating an ET?" I understand. I've even caught myself thinking this way at times. An investment of time and energy is required in order to improve a team. Is it worth it? Yes, it is worth it. Consider these factors illustrating the value of extraordinary teams:

- Unified teams are 2900% more likely to produce great work, 2000% more likely to enjoy work, 175% more likely to plan to stay for at least six years and 96% less likely to experience burnout.[6] These numbers seem a bit extreme, like I'm exaggerating. I'm not.
- **Extraordinary teams are expected at big companies.** Google has spent millions of dollars looking to improve their team performance. Teams are researched at Disney. Pepsi has a person dedicated to organizational development with the expectation of increasing individual and team performance. I've even been hired by movie theaters to help increase team performance. A person who can unite a group and create an ET has a future. Even if it's not measured as explicitly as we will in this book, companies are expecting it and looking for it on resumes. I believe that leaders and organizations that consistently produce low to average results will eventually become less prominent because high-performing and ETs are already becoming more mainstream.
- **ETs are fun.** Members of ETs truly enjoy their time on the team. They can come from all different backgrounds and experiences, but when they reach that level of unity, they learn to celebrate differences instead of setting them aside. Every person—100% of the people I researched who had been on an ET—used the word "family." They enjoyed being around each other. They were comfortable together— and happy at work. A good time was created for all.
- **ETs produce results.** If you need a project to excel, if you need creativity, if you need a new process or a new product, clear the path for ETs. They will surpass all expectations and then some. Their energy seems endless. Participation in a team like this is mentally invigorating. Team members feed off each other's energy. They think about work outside of work because they want to, not because they have to. Work is exciting for this group of people.
- **ETs experience spillover success outside of work.** When people are on a great team, their participation tends to improve their work life. They are happier at work. They show up on time or early. They call in sick less. They volunteer for extra work. Because they're happier at work, they tend to be happier at home. That happiness spills over as resilience and a greater ability to problem-solve when dealing with the stresses of home and social life. Because they are arrive home happier, they also tend to be a better brother/sister, mother/ father, son/daughter, husband/wife, partner, friend or volunteer. Do you see how this happiness will help improve their home life? And

the happiness is released via a two-way valve; when their home lives improve, they tend to arrive at work happier. Because these people are happier at work, they perform better and are less likely to quit, more likely to be committed to the organization, far more likely to be creative, etc. It's not that their struggles disappear. When people have something as positive as being a part of an ET in their lives, they tend to face the problems with a different outlook. I call this the *upward spiral effect* of awesome teams.

- **ET members stay connected.** This was a surprising find. I noticed a trend when people were reflecting back on their great teams. They tended to still be in touch with many of them decades later. When people reflected back on poor or average teams, they rarely stayed in touch with any of their team members. One vice president I interviewed pointed out a mechanic on the floor. He said, "See that guy right there. That's Bill [not his real name]. He was on that emergency team we were talking about earlier. I make it a point to swing by anytime I'm in the area." The team he was referring to was formed more than 15 years prior when the vice president was still a senior manager. For more than 15 years, he still made a point to at least say hello to his old friend from his previous ET. Many junior high and high school teachers I spoke with who had created extraordinary classrooms stayed in touch with their students even after college graduation. Team members from ETs tend to become permanent connections in each other's social networks.

- **ETs benefit from collective intelligence.** Putting a group of people together doesn't mean that group will make better decisions. In fact, at times, a group can actually make worse decisions. But when that group has open communication, trusts each other and is focused on a goal, the team members benefit from an increase in collective intelligence. Nineteenth century poet and philosopher Ralph Waldo Emerson wrote many letters and articles centered on becoming a transcendent person. In a letter titled *Greatness*, he quipped, "Shall I tell you the secret of the true scholar? It is this: Every man I meet is my master in some point, and in that I learn of him." This is the feeling among an ET. There is no one greater than the other. Everyone is each other's master in something. Everyone tries to learn from each other, and thus they are all edified. When this happens in a group, it is called *collective intelligence*. This occurs when the intelligence of a group is greater than that of a single person, but this only happens when the group chooses to share and learn from each other.

Larry Michaelson, emeritus professor of management at the University of Oklahoma and author of many books and articles on group learning, discovered the importance of collective intelligence during his decades as an educator. He learned that when students work together on assignments that require creativity and problem-solving, the students are more engaged, retain the information longer and have an improved outlook on education in general. Based on his experience and research, he created Team-Based Learning theory.[7] I use many of its components in my classroom and trainings.

- Extraordinary groups benefit from collective intelligence, learning from others in the group, and they tend to retain the information. In other words, everyone leaves the team more intelligent than before, a key for people looking to create a learning culture in their organization.

How Extraordinary Teams Are Born

The benefits of being on an ET are outstanding, so the next question is, how do they form? There is plenty of evidence that they exist, and I had learned how amazing they were through books and numerous interviews and observations—but I hadn't quite figured out how they formed. As with many teams, and as noted in many books on team, there are numerous variables that contribute to team success. In pursuit of an answer, I continued my research. A colleague recommended a book called *Hot Groups* by Leavitt and Lipman-Blumen,[8] which I referenced in the preface. The book outlined several variables that were specific to the extremely high-performing groups I was studying.

Jean Lipman-Blumen received her PhD from Harvard in social relations, then completed a postdoc at Carnegie Mellon and Stanford University. She served as assistant director of the National Institute of Education under President Jimmy Carter. She researched the functionality of groups and by 1999 had more than 50 published scholarly articles, many of which focused on group dynamics. Her books, *Connective Edge* and *Connective Leadership*, were both nominated for a Pulitzer Prize.

Her husband, Harold J. Leavitt, received his PhD from MIT and was a true pioneer in managerial psychology. His textbook *Managerial Psychology* was the first of its kind. It challenged the traditional structure of corporations in the 1950s and moved to shift the focus of power and authority to relationships and development. For many decades, it was one of the top-selling textbooks in its field, going through five editions and selling hundreds of thousands of copies. His book *Corporate Pathfinders* highlighted the traits and behaviors of the early trailblazers of business and was a standard in business book collections. He also published dozens of articles on organizational leadership and corporate structure.

The two moved to Pasadena, California, and joined Peter Drucker and other key business researchers. It was during one of their conversations between scholars that the idea came up for *Hot Groups*, groups of people who seemed to excel beyond expectations. Jean and John's research uncovered hot groups in a wide variety of fields in many different industries, as had mine up to this point. She introduced the world to these tremendous teams and compiled a list of ingredients to making hot groups work. Their book was published in 1999 and was nominated as "Best Business Book" by the American Publishers Association. Following is a list Jean and John laid out in their book of the four main ingredients to create a hot group:

1. **Culture.** The culture of the organization or department needs to be one that allows for teams to grow. It needs to be a culture of innovation and growth. ETs are exceptionally fast at accomplishing work. They need space and support to move quickly as they create and develop their ideas. A negative culture restricts ETs from reaching their full potential, according to the authors.

    I had issue with this claim because I did see ETs appear in negative cultures.

2. **Timing.** Hot groups seemed to appear when they were needed, according to the authors. When a company needed an ET to help them out of a bind, for example, one would appear.

    The interesting thing to me about timing is that an ET isn't initially recognized, until they are churning out success. Many times, ETs and Hot Groups are formed and performing without the company realizing it. When the success is being documented, that's when the company suddenly recognizes the team and tends to say, "We were facing a tremendous challenge. Luckily, a great team appeared just in time." Well, yeah, but the team was already there. Maybe what they should say is, "We've found the best team we never knew we needed."

3. **Resources.** *Hot Groups* mentions that large amounts of resources are needed but later says that extraordinary groups tend to find their own resources.

    I've found that access to the right resources at the right time is more important than providing a mountain of resources all at once. Providing a team unlimited resources doesn't necessarily provide the proper grounds for a tremendous team. Often ETs don't even know what they're going to need at first because they don't know the direction they plan to go until it happens. And many times, they make an unexpected pivot in a new direction, shifting their resource requirement. One thing is certain, though: When ETs are rushing forward, what they need most is administrative support for accessing resources. That is the most vital resource. With the proper levels of support, the team will find and obtain the resources—but they need the right support in order to gain the permissions to get the resources they need.

4. **Freedom.** This is something the authors of *Hot Groups* definitely had right. Teams need the freedom and trust from the organization and leadership to go in the direction they see fit. This doesn't mean that guidance cannot be provided, but the team needs the freedom to create and execute the project based on how they envision it. To the team, their project is their art.

The Art of Team Performance

I love art. I'm in fact passionate about it. Yet art is far more than just paintings and performances. Art is everywhere. For me, a well-run business is art. A smoothly run event is art.

Art is a celebration of excellence. We admire the creativity and skill required to paint and sculpt. That's part of why we love it—because it involves someone pushing one's potential to create something new. We marvel and ask, "How did she do that?" as we look at the modern sculpture by the new emerging artist in our city—or "How did he think that was possible?" when we admire Michelangelo's masterpieces.

That's how I feel about business. It's the creative palate for many innovative thinkers. It's that potential that keeps me awake some nights. I love it.v

For an ET, their project is their art. They are creating something and watching it come together piece by piece. They're putting their energy and devotion into this project. They take great pride and ownership in the outcome, as if it were their masterpiece.

Unfortunately, some organizations have so many restrictions in place that artists do not feel like they can create. They require the artist to go through a chain of approvals or administrators, each with the ability to make changes to the project.

Imagine Picasso being told, "You must only paint from one perspective." His revolutionary cubism would never have come to light, drawing millions to view his work even well after his death.

Team performance, too, requires us to view team members as needing some creative license.

But frequently, an organization often feels the need to add their own objectives and requirements to the project. While some level of oversight or input by those outside the project may be inherent or necessary (as we will discuss shortly), as weird as this might sound to some, too much involvement can hurt the artist. Too many requirements and changes transform the project into someone else's. It isn't the team's creation anymore.

I once discussed this with an administrator who was guilty of restricting his team in such a way. He said, "But John, I will do whatever they ask me to do. Just tell me how to do it, and I will." His heart was in the right place, but would you tell Leonardo to hand you the paintbrush? "Leo, I will paint whatever you want me to paint. Just tell me what to paint." It's not that simple. You would want Leonardo's passion, expertise, hand, eye for detail and vision for the project. It is Leonardo's name on the painting. He should be the one to paint it. ETs need the freedom to excel. A better statement by this administrator could have been: "I wouldn't dream of asking them to let me do the project for them. But I do let them know I support them and will provide any resources they need to get it done."

A quick note about administrative regulations: Just as it is Leonardo's name on the painting, it also belongs to the organization funding the project. The organization needs to make sure the project meets their quality and safety standards. Requirements and administrative approvals exist to make sure poor projects are made into good ones. Unfortunately, this also means that excellent projects could risk being brought down to good if those same regulations limit innovation. Sometimes the mold needs to be broken to create something great. There is no single answer to this. Both parties need to understand and communicate their needs. In other words, organizational administrators should be partners, not dictators. A team should feel free to reach out to the administrators if they feel any regulations are limiting to their ultimate outcome.

Expanding on the Findings of *Hot Groups*

Hot Groups was a great read, but it didn't tell the complete story of ETs.

The authors had identified many wonderful teams that shared many excellent traits. The teams described in the book used words like "family" and "magic" when discussing teamwork. They had fun, laughed and seemed to live for work. They loved the challenge. *Hot Groups* was describing what I called ETs! I was ecstatic by the discovery! Such an accomplished team of writers and researchers had shared the same interest as me. Page after page, I highlighted—until I realized there was no point in highlighting. I wanted to highlight everything!

I hung on every word—until the end of the book, when John and Jean announced that *hot groups were random.* As previously discussed, this was a tremendous letdown to me. I realized that what I was researching was a continuation of the concepts within *Hot Groups*—not a part 1 but rather a new direction.

As I mentioned in the preface, I had a chance to speak with Jean Lipmen-Blumen in 2015. By this time in her career, she had published three more books, won several more awards and published approximately 100 more articles than when she wrote *Hot Groups*. Her enthusiasm for the topic had not waned one bit. She was thrilled to discuss hot groups. We dissected the topic for over an hour. Her mind was sharp, remembering tiny details from her book. She quizzed me on my findings. We celebrated shared results. I told her about the next step I wanted to take in my research—to expand her findings, pointing out that hot groups were not random but completely unified groups. She loved it.

My findings actually support her decades of research on social organizations. She gave me her full blessing to continue the work of *Hot Groups*, a topic she said she probably should have continued researching.

At the end of the conversation, I noted her obvious enthusiasm for the topic and inquired why she had stopped moving forward if she loved the topic so much. She discussed her time at the Claremont Graduate School and how she was working with tremendous researchers. They would meet and discuss topics on a regular basis. *Hot Groups* was one of those topics. They studied it for a couple years, but then another topic would come up, then another. There were so many topics, she admitted that some did not receive the full attention that they deserved.

So, with Jean Lipmen-Blumen's blessing, I hoped to devote the attention to this topic that it was due.

Unity Is the Key

After compiling more than a decade's worth of research and reviewing notes from interviews, observations, articles, books and projects, the answer to me is clear: *the key to extraordinary groups is unity.*

One hundred percent of the extraordinary groups I studied were extremely unified in purpose. They were often described as being of "one heart, one mind." They were committed to each other and to the success of the team.

The lowest performing groups were not unified at all. They were selfish, uncaring toward fellow members and untrusting, and they had their own agendas. They fought and were not committed to the goals of the team.

As long as the basic requirements are met, *unity* is the number one contributor of team performance, based on the extensive research I have done on team performance.

The United States of America was founded on this principle—that if the states, a disjointed group of townships and provinces, could come together and act with one accord, then they would be unstoppable.

The Revolutionary War ended in 1784, but the states didn't really start forming into a country until many years later. Many states even maintained their own currency. The purpose of the Bill of Rights was to create some common ground between governance at the state and federal level.

Similarly, the purpose of The League of Nations and later the United Nations was to approach the world problems together, as a united front against political and economic dangers. It can definitely be said that United Nations and the United States aren't as united as they once were, but the point is that there is strength in unity.

When a group is united in purpose and in plan, fully committed to achieving success, there is little that they cannot accomplish.

After a few more years reviewing notes from past interviews and continuing to conduct interviews and work with teams, I noticed four common themes continued to pop up. I will refer to them in this book as the components of unity. They can be identified by many different names, but I refer to them as

1. Focus,
2. Direction,
3. Trust and
4. Conflict.

Focus is dedication and commitment to a goal. Top teams have clear goals—and clear commitment to accomplishing those goals.

Direction is clear strategy for how to accomplish those goals. Top-performing teams I studied not only had a strategy but were also 100% committed to executing that strategy.

Trust. There are several types of trust. The trust we're referring to is *social trust*. *Social trust* is the measure of a team's willingness to share ideas, feelings and feedback with each other, without fear of repercussion or judgement. It involves having the ability to be your whole self— expressing creativity together.

Finally, the first three components discussed contribute to unity, but the last one, *conflict*, is a destroyer of unity. I mentioned it because it is noticeably absent from the highest performing teams and obviously present in the lowest performing team. It can bring a team's performance down so quickly that I couldn't write a book about unity without including it. Task conflict is when two or more people disagree with how a project should be completed. Task conflict is normal and very often helpful and important to innovation, but *relational conflict* occurs when two people don't like each other. Relational conflict is the great vacuum of success. It is a unity destroyer. When relational conflict is present, performance plummets.

You may ask why one of these factors, conflict, sounds negative and the rest are positive. The inclusion of relational conflict was very intentional. It is that severe. It is a warning. Recently, someone gave me directions to a place I wanted to visit. After receiving directions, I was then warned that the weather would be bad and to look out going in one particular area where wrecks were frequent. Consider *focus*, *direction* and *trust* the path to increasing unity while *relational conflict* is the bad weather and dangerous intersections I want you to avoid.

We will tackle the topic of relational conflict holistically so that you are equipped to manage it successfully on a team. Its place as a component of unity is important, since it dictates how a team can proceed.

- These four components are the core makeup of unity—when a group of people get together and commit to a goal, establish a direction, trust each other and successfully manage relational conflict.
- Maximize the focus, direction and trust.
- Minimize conflict.

Every team malady and dysfunction can be tied to one or more of these four components.

Extraordinary Teams Are "Out of This World"

I respect the name *hot groups*, originally coined by Jean and John, but I decided to use a different term. Hot groups, as described by Jean and John, were temporary, short-lived. The ETs I saw rarely cooled before their task was completed, unless acted upon by an outside force. Multiple groups I worked with remained at extraordinary levels for more than a year, much longer than the more task-focused hot groups described in the book.

Additionally, the term "groups" implies several people that work mostly independent of each other. ETs work inter-dependently. They need each other for energy and reinforcement. They feed off of each other's excitement. They enjoy being together.

I even like that ETs share the same abbreviation as an extraterrestrial—an homage to one person that described his ET experience as "out of this world." Hopefully, ETs become so commonplace among organizations that they no longer feel extraordinary but that ETs just become teams, the norm. In fact, we will start referring to them as ETs at this point in the book.

So, after hearing all of these great things, who wants to be a part of an ET? When I ask this in a presentation, nearly every hand is raised. I have never once gotten, "Yeah, but no. It's not for me. Thank you, though." Everyone seems to want to be on a team like this—or at least improve their current and future team situations.

So, what's the hold-up? If the desire is there, then why don't we see more great and ETs? I believe it's because of what the "Fishing Ninja" said earlier: You have to know how to correctly use the right lures at the right times. The hope is that this book will help teach you how to be your own team consultant—where you will be able to analyze your team, seeing where you might be lacking so you can apply appropriate fixes.

You may be thinking, "Hmm, high hopes and easy shifts that will change my life? I've heard this before. This author is a blind optimist like all the others, promising a better world without actually having lived in our current one." Let me address this thought for you before we proceed, so you see that I understand why you may think this, while respectfully disagreeing.

Because of the success I had in manufacturing, I used to be a regular presenter at Texas Christian University's Leadership Academy. I spoke on "The Top 3 Things Every Leader Should Know." Normally, when I finished speaking, I received a great round of applause and was asked many simple questions about what books I read or what my favorite music was (college students want to know these things).

At the end of one of my presentations, I presented the very early stages of my research on unity. I opened it up for Q&A at the end. I received the usual questions, but then I was surprised by one negative comment: "This all seems like rainbows and butterflies. Wouldn't you say you're some sort of super optimist?" The hosting professor's eyes shot up, and he looked at me slightly embarrassed. I welcomed the unexpected challenge, but it really caught me off guard.

I thought about that a second. I had never considered myself a super optimist. *Was it just my predisposition to look at positive scenarios that clouded my judgement regarding teams?* After a few seconds' pause to gather my thoughts from such an unexpected question, the answer clicked. "No, not at all." I replied. "I wouldn't call myself an optimist. I'd call myself a *realist*. I've seen this work. I've applied these principles myself and coached others to do the same. We have seen tremendous results. This is real. These are not made-up results." He nodded his head and later thanked me for my sincere comment.

My response was true. I have seen the concepts I will share with you actually work. I have interviewed hundreds of people, worked with well over 100 teams in many industries and read countless books and articles on the subject. I've used the principles myself and coached leaders at all levels with great success.

The takeaway for you is this: In each scenario and environment I've seen, these concepts work. I expect them to work for you as well.

Notes

1. Brody, J. E. (2017, June 12). Social interaction is critical for mental and physical health. *The New York Times.* www.nytimes.com/2017/06/12/well/live/having-friends-is-good-for-you.html

2. Brody, J. E. (2017, June 12). Social interaction is critical for mental and physical health. *The New York Times*. www.nytimes.com/2017/06/12/well/live/having-friends-is-good-for-you.html
3. DeWall, C. N., & Bushman, B. J. (2011). Social acceptance and rejection: The sweet and the bitter. *Current Directions in Psychological Science*, *20*(4), 256–260.
4. Strack, R. et al. (2021, January 24). Decoding global talent. *BCG Global*. www.bcg.com/publications/2014/people-organization-human-resources-decoding-global-talent
5. Martin, J. (2018, December 17). Depression reduced by social BELONGING, feelings of inclusion. *Psychiatry Advisor*. www.psychiatryadvisor.com/home/topics/mood-disorders/depressive-disorder/depression-reduced-by-social-belonging-feelings-of-inclusion/
6. Tanner Institute, O. C. (2021). (rep.). 2022 global culture report. OC Tanner Institute. Retrieved from www.octanner.com/content/dam/oc-tanner/images/v2/culture-report/2022/home/INT-GCR2022.pdf
7. Michaelsen, L. K., Knight, A. B., & Fink, L. D. (2004). Team-based learning: A transformative use of small groups in college teaching. Centers for Teaching and Technology—Book Library, 199. https://digitalcommons.georgiasouthern.edu/ct2-library/199
8. Lipman-Blumen, J., & Leavitt, H. J. (2001). *Hot groups: Seeding them, feeding them, and using them to ignite your organization*. Oxford University Press.

Chapter 2

Important Considerations for Team Success

As suggested in the discussion of *Hot Groups*,[1] the concepts in this book will challenge several beliefs held by many regarding teams. There are a few key beliefs that need to be challenged up front before we can move on. Hopefully, this will be review for many of you, but I want to be sure to challenge these beliefs up front because these views I challenge here may prevent growth in learning about the makeup of team unity.

After observing and studying teams for more than a decade in various industries and interviewing countless team members and leaders, I discovered that their feelings and beliefs about teams were similar depending on how successful their previous teams had been. Here are some common beliefs they shared:

- New teams with new people tended to have hopeful outlooks on their success.
- Those who had previously experienced a majority of failures or lackluster results tended to be less hopeful about team success, believing that their current team would achieve similar poor results, especially if the team was organized by a familiar leader or filled with familiar teammates.
- Those who had been on an ET prior were more hopeful, especially if their leader had previously been on an ET. They were less hopeful if their leader had previously struggled to achieve success.

The beliefs of these groups will be discussed further and in more detail later. The point is that there are two beliefs that had to be established before their teams would see any noticeable improvements. All ETs maintain these beliefs. They are vital for a team to increase its unity. The two listed below are important to remember as we go throughout this book because they will influence your learning about unity and may challenge your beliefs on teams.

1. Team unity exists on a scale. It is not a light switch.
2. Talent is *not* the number one contributor to team success.

DOI: 10.4324/9781003269038-4

Team Success Exists on a Scale

In just a few pages, we will dive into the four contributors of team unity—which are crucial in determining a team's success. Before we do, it's important to realize one of the key points of this book: that every team has some measure of all four of the components unity.

As we stated in the last chapter, contrary to what some team books teach, team success is not binary. It is not a light switch that is on or off, a good team or a bad team. While some authors may preach that you either have it or you don't, I've found that team success exists on a continuum. It's not an on or off switch but rather can fluctuate over time. And the best news is, as a leader, you have the power to influence the level of success your team achieves.

The same can be said of unity. Think of a 1 to 10 scale, where 1 is the least unified team and 10 is the highest. Many believe that a team is either a 1 or a 10, but there are many points in between that we'll discuss later when we introduce The Unity Formula.

Whatever level of success you currently have on your team, you have an opportunity to grow by applying the principles of unity. That's the good news; you don't have to strive for perfection in order to make a marked improvement in your team's performance. Moving a team from a 1 to a 5 or a 3 to a 7 in unity would be tremendous improvement. This is a transformational way to look at teams.

Too often teams are looked at as either successful or not, strong or not, cohesive or not. Like the Fishing Ninja example used earlier, teams don't just perform or not perform—just as fish aren't just hungry or not. Teams, like fish, are always hungry, always ready to achieve. They're just waiting for the right lure.

This point is vital to understand because as leaders, believing that there is no hope for a team can decrease morale and the critical investment of energy and time that is required to move a team up the scale. Also, correctly identifying where a team falls on a scale can help you apply the appropriate "lure" to grow their unity and success. They perform on a scale based on how unified they are. Every team has the potential to be great, even extraordinary. Each team just falls at a different part of the scale.

Imagine if coaches believed teams were binary in success, either good or not, without any hope of improvement. Imagine the press conferences:

I'd like to thank everyone that came out to see us today. Thank you to my assistant coaches. They've been great. Thank you to so many people. Alright, I gathered you here today to let you know that our team is terrible. Please, please hold your questions until the end. See, our team is just not good this year. I was just dealt a rough hand. Don't expect much from us. We'll probably squeeze out a game or two, but that's about it. Hopefully, many of these players will finally leave the team so we can actually recruit a list of all-stars and finally have a chance. Now, I'll take your questions. . . .

Would anyone accept that as an excuse? What if a teacher said a child was just *how they were* and couldn't amount to more? What if a retail manager said his/her store would never amount to anything more than it was currently performing? This sounds ridiculous as you read it, but many people make excuses for their teams, giving a list of reasons why their team will always perform low or average. Why do we accept this? We shouldn't because we are humans capable of accomplishing great things.

Mountains of research show that we want our leaders to believe in us and lead us to new heights. Companies seek these types of leaders and are willing to pay them a great deal of money. One of the top resume attributes desired by recruiters is *leadership*.[2] Recruiters seek people who have the potential to successfully lead a team to accomplish goals.[3] Candidates identified as having such potential are often introduced to the firm's leadership development program so they can receive even more instruction and responsibility—and improve the firm's bottom line.[4]

The point is we shouldn't accept the idea that a team is the way it is just because that's how it is. Abandon that idea. Every team is somewhere on the *unity scale* and therefore has potential to move up the scale to an extraordinary level. Not most teams, not a lot of teams. *Every* team is on the scale, and *every* team can be improved. Keep this in mind as we continue through the four components of team unity.

Talent Is Not the Number One Contributor to Team Success

One of the most common questions I get as I discuss team unity—and The Unity Formula—is about talent. Just recently at a presentation, someone commented, "Yeah, but at some point, none of this [unity] matters if you have star performers on your team."

If this is your belief, I understand. I even believed as you did before I began my research, but now I strongly disagree.

First, let's discuss the idea of a "star performer." Star performers received their reputation for outperforming their peers. So, the general idea is that if we put a room full of star performers on a team, we will have tremendous success. Strong hypothesis, but it isn't necessarily true.

More than 100 years ago, Lord Shackleton, an accomplished Arctic explorer, set out to do what no one had done on foot: reach the South Pole. Lord Shackleton had the experience and ambition to accomplish such a feat. Finding investors in the adventure required little effort. The hope was that Britain would soon lead the exploration race.

The next step was to hire a crew. Imagine the task of hiring a crew for an expedition such as this. The timing was 40 years before Sir Edmund Hillary peaked Mount Everest. Radio communication was new and had yet to extend to Antarctica; thus, the group would have zero communication with the outside world. Flight was still relatively new. The population was only half of what it is today and still largely centered on cities. The automobile had been invented but was only just starting to be mass produced. Compared with today's standards and technology in cartography and equipment, these were primitive times in exploration.

The crew would need to face Earth's harshest climate, the worst weather conditions and countless other dangers that accompanied a constantly shifting continent. The trek would be hundreds of miles, mostly walking. Three dog teams were provided, but those were to carry the provisions. The crew would need to walk and sleep in freezing temperatures while being wet—whether from sweat or ocean spray. The members of this crew would need to depend on each other for their survival.

You, as the crew leader, would need to depend on your crew, not only for your survival but also for the success of your journey. Your reputation would depend on it.

Imagine the type of crew you might want on such an adventure. Bear Ghrylls, Dual Survivalists and other celebrity outdoor professionals might stand out. You might ask for a resume and list of references. You might even be wise to ask for a demonstration of knowledge.

It might surprise you, as it did me, to learn that Lord Shackleton hired each of his expedition team members with nothing more than a five-minute interview.[5] Lord Shackleton believed within five minutes, he'd know if he could depend on that person for team success and survival, whether they had experience or not. In fact, many of the men had never been on an expedition such as this before. Skills and talent were not his top priority. The number one criteria for joining his expedition was *a willingness to commit to the group—and to the goal.*

It isn't uncommon in today's management to hire for attitude before talent. Elon Musk frequently claims that while minimum abilities are required, ultimately he is looking for someone who can commit to the mission of the organization, someone willing to sacrifice themselves for the ultimate goal of creating, developing and implementing some of the world's most innovative designs.[6] IDEO, a design and consulting firm, follows a similar strategy for hiring their small staff of professionals. They hire psychologists, teachers, engineers, artists and more for their product design firm. They believe the key is that a person is creative and willing to give their all. After that, they'll learn everything else.[7]

I found a similar response when working with one of the world's top engineering and manufacturing companies. I found people with business and engineering degrees—along with degrees in opera, Spanish, theater, music, general studies and more. They all worked side by side in similar jobs. The company hired for heart and commitment, not necessarily for the degree they had obtained. They understood that team success is not about the degree you have; it's about passion and willingness to make change as a team.

Attitude and hard work surpassing talent as a top criteria is true for students as well. I worked with a teacher at an extremely low socio-economic school that had 92% free or reduced lunch, yet within a year, this teacher had taken the lowest testing group of sixth graders in the history of the school and turned them into reading and writing masters, testing in the 90th percentile in the nation. The teacher replicated the results the following year. These students were not the cream of the crop with white-collared parents or private-school educated students with many resources for learning and development at home. Their parents were unemployed, underemployed or never home because they were working more than one low-wage job. No one had even heard of the school until this achievement.

Superstars can be a great addition to a team, but disunity will greatly limit the success of any superstar team. Unity is needed to reach a team's full potential.

A Tale of Two Teams

Disunity and talent can lead to disaster. Sometimes people that have all the talent in the world should be unified for a great cause yet unfortunately are not. The result is sometimes disastrous.

On January 28, 1986, the nation experienced a tremendous tragedy. The *Challenger* shuttle exploded just 73 seconds into the launch. The shuttle was staffed with a team of well-trained astronauts, and Christa McAuliffe, a social studies teacher from New Hampshire was set to be the first ordinary citizen in space. All seven people on board were killed in the accident.

NASA was staffed with the best and the brightest—truly a team of all-stars with degrees from the country's top universities. Most were launch veterans with years of experience at NASA in various capacities. The failure was not because of a lack of talent. The failure was due to a simple O-ring, which became brittle when cold and allowed a fuel leak.[8] You might suspect that something like that was not the ground team's, flight team's or design team's fault. It was the fault of the O-ring, right? The manufacturers, part of the ground team, knew about the defect. So did the NASA managers. It is believed that others knew about it as well, but the decision was made to continue forth with the launch.[9]

It is difficult to understand today how important the *Challenger* news was in 1986. Today, the news is filled with so much drama that much of the details of what happens day to day are often ignored. We may even be a bit desensitized to news today. In 1986, America wasn't flooded with information like today—especially when it comes to space launches. America had been traveling to space for less than 30 years. The idea of space travel was still captivating. Hundreds and sometimes thousands of people would show up for a launch, especially this one with a "normal person"—Christa. All the news stations would dedicate programming to the launch. The world took notice.

The launch was already delayed six days due to weather. News crews would call incessantly hoping to hear that the launch was a go. Delaying the launch to repair O-rings that may or may not be a problem to the launch would cause problems to the program.[10] A few of the team members abandoned one of the keys of unity: focus. Instead of understanding and remaining completely committed to safety, one of NASA's most crucial foundational principals,[11] some of the team members lost their focus and decided that public relations (PR) was more important.

There are lots of stories of little league teams, city basketball teams, intern program teams, families, businesses and more. Stories of teams today and in history. Many movies have been made and books have been written. They often share the same plot: a group of people who were not the greatest of their time got together and accomplished amazing results.

Here's another far more common theme found in a more basic story. An employee of a top manufacturing company shared a story of when he was on an extraordinary team (ET). Josh was excited to start his new internship, but he was a bit nervous. He was starting with a very large company, with more than 10,000 people in one plant. He was nervous.[12]

On the day he arrived, Josh was shown around, introduced to his group and put into an area where the other interns in his work group were seated in their cubicles. He enjoyed getting to know them, all from different parts of the country, different schools and different majors. After a few days of onboarding meetings and introductions, the group of interns was given a project to work on for the duration of their internships. The initial response from the group of interns was disbelief.

"We didn't know anything. We had only just learned where the restroom was. We had no clue how we were going to figure this out." They did all have one strong point in common, however: They wanted to impress their boss. After the shock wore off, they got to work at step one, learning about the project.[13]

This is a key point about ETs. They often don't know how to get to their goals, but they know enough to take the next few steps. Josh's group of colleagues went forward, asking around, learning as much as they could. Eventually, they learned about a host of problems, more than just the ones the boss had pointed out. They began making lists, finding solutions, continually learning and growing. Their energy was contagious. They motivated each other. They had very little distractions. They were generally left alone. They came in early, worked late and hung out on the weekends. They could see their progress. Any issue was handled as a team; low quality was not an option. They dreamed about working together, everyone getting offers at the end of the internship.

At the end of the summer, after countless hours, they presented their findings. The bosses were impressed with this team of go-getters. Their results far exceeded expectations. They all received offers. Many accepted.

The intern example was not the norm for the company. Most intern groups stuck to the status quo, delivering exactly what was asked of them. This group went above—and way beyond.

The difference between the NASA example and the intern example is this:

- The NASA team had unbelievable talent complete with competence and intelligence. The NASA team allowed competing interests—losing focus on safety and instead opted to allow PR pressure to dictate decisions—to get in the way of mission success.
- The intern team had very little knowledge or know-how, but they had a thirst for knowledge and wanted to succeed. They worked together to make sure they did. They remained unified throughout the project.

Sports provides an abundance of examples, as I've mentioned. Many basketball coaches, including Larry Bird,[14] Pat Riley[15] and Phil Jackson,[16] have all admitted that superstars do not make the team. In fact, superstar teams are the cause of many disasters in sports history—and even in world history. Talent, while excellent to have, is therefore not the key to the success of a team.

This isn't to say that a team of unified fifth graders can run a Fortune 100 to extreme success. Yet as long as a minimum requirement of knowledge or skill is met for task accomplishment, a team's unity—as defined by the components outlined in this book—is the overall most powerful determining factor of performance. Professional coaches and teamwork authors have been talking about different parts of unity for decades—and now it's time to explore how it works in any team, including in business.

No matter how much talent is on a team, if the team cannot unify and work together, then performance will suffer. When a team embodies the four components of unity, they can slide up the scale of The Unity Formula and achieve greatness.

Notes

1. Lipman-Blumen, J., & Leavitt, H. J. (2001). *Hot groups: Seeding them, feeding them, and using them to ignite your organization.* Oxford University Press.
2. Zenger, J. (2015, January 15). Great leaders can double profits, research shows. *Forbes Magazine.* www.forbes.com/sites/jackzenger/2015/01/15/great-leaders-can-double-profits-research-shows/?sh=195459896ca6
3. Indeed Editorial Team. (2020, December 1). Top 11 skills employers look for in candidates. Indeed Career Guide. www.indeed.com/career-advice/resumes-cover-letters/skills-employers-look-for/
4. Corsey, M. (2021, July 12). Leadership training can pay huge dividends for midsize companies. *Harvard Business Review*, Harvard Business Publishing. hbr.org/2021/07/leadership-training-can-pay-huge-dividends-for-midsize-companies
5. Lansing, A. (2015). *Endurance: Shackleton's incredible voyage.* Basic Books.
6. Burgersdijk, M. (2020, May 25). What I learned from Elon musk in SELECTING top talent at Tesla. LinkedIn. www.linkedin.com/pulse/what-i-learned-from-elon-musk-selecting-top-talent-burgersdijk/
7. Zhou, D. What I Look for. . . . IDEO.org, IDEO. www.ideo.org/perspective/what-i-look-for
8. Mcdonald, A. J. (2012). *Truth, lies, and O-rings: Inside the space shuttle "Challenger" disaster.* University Press of Florida.
9. Mcdonald, A. J. (2012). *Truth, lies, and O-rings: Inside the space shuttle "Challenger" disaster.* University Press of Florida.
10. Mcdonald, A. J. (2012). *Truth, lies, and O-rings: Inside the space shuttle "Challenger" disaster.* University Press of Florida.
11. Blodgett, R. (2018, April 20). Our missions and values. NASA. www.nasa.gov/careers/our-mission-and-values
12. Ross, J. (2013, March 25). Josh's first experience as an Intern.
13. Ross, J. (2013, March 25). Josh's first experience as an Intern.
14. Bird, L., & MacMullan, J. (1999). *Bird watching: On playing and coaching the game I love.* Warner Books.
15. Riley, P. (1994). *The winner within: A life plan for team players.* Berkley Books.
16. Jackson, P., & Delehanty, H. (2014). *Eleven rings: The soul of success.* Penguin Press.

Part 2

Defining Unity

Introducing the Four Components of Unity

Unity is the number one contributing factor to higher performing teams. How then do we create unity in teams?

Creating more team unity begins by understanding the four components that compose it. Simply put, unity is created when a team *understands and is fully committed to achieving a goal, develops and is committed to executing a strategy, socially trusts each other and minimizes relational conflict.*

As I stated in Part 1, I will simplify these four key components as *focus, direction, trust* and *conflict.*

A team may have lower levels of all four of these or may even excel at one of the four. Based on my research and practice, they must have high levels of focus, direction and trust and low levels of conflict to achieve the level of team unity necessary to become an extraordinary team.

You may find yourself skeptical, asking questions like

- How does *conflict* fit in a model about unity? Isn't conflict a bad thing?
- Isn't *focus* pretty similar to *direction*? Why do you need both?
- What does *trust* really mean, and why do you think you can measure it?

Don't worry; we will address all of these questions. For now, I simply want you to understand the premise that these four components are what comprise unity within teams.

Here is a brief description of each component. We will delve into the implications of each of these throughout the book.

- **Focus:** how well people understand and are committed to the goal
- **Direction:** how well people understand and are committed to the plan

DOI: 10.4324/9781003269038-5

- **Trust:** how well people socially trust those around them
- **Conflict:** the amount of relational conflict in the group

Each component within your team's unity is measured on a 1–10 scale, depending on where people fall—which we will explore shortly. The score for each is then placed into The Unity Formula explained later in the book. This formula can then be used as a guide to increase unity with your group or organization.

$$((Focus \times Direction) + 2 \times Trust)$$

Conflict

Look and sound confusing? It's actually a simple and useful management tool I've used many, many times with great success. The following chapters first describe the importance of each of the four components, then explain how to measure the components on a 1–10 scale. This is followed by how to use the scale with The Unity Formula and suggestions on how to improve each component. Rest assured: It'll be explained in detail with examples in the upcoming chapters.

Chapter 3

Unity Component #1—Focus

We've all heard quotes like this from famous players and coaches—about a group of people who really want "it."

> *If I had one or two guys who didn't care about winning, it wouldn't make it worthwhile for me. I'm just lucky I have this collection of players who really want it. Too often these days, it seems the NBA has a group of guys with too much going on. That's what people don't realize. If one guy is off, it can affect the whole team.*
> —Larry Bird, 1999[1]

But what is the *it* that they want? The *it* is to win and to do what it takes to win. In order to achieve unity, your team must be clear about their goal—and united in going after it. That is what I refer to as *focus*.

Focus is critical to mission success. Before any team can move forward, the team must know where it is going. Whether it's a state championship, creating a new widget to solve a problem or ending world hunger, your team must unite with focus around that goal.

- Focus is split into two parts: understanding the goal and commitment to goal attainment. *Understanding the goal* means they know what they are achieving together.
- *Commitment* means they will work collaboratively until they get it done.

> *When you're surrounded by people who share a passionate commitment around a common purpose, anything is possible.*
> —Howard Schultz, former CEO of Starbucks

When a team member understands the goal and is fully committed to achieving it, they are willing to sacrifice time, energy, meals, outside

DOI: 10.4324/9781003269038-6

contact—anything. If team members are not committed, then they will allow other tasks to take precedence from the goals of the team.

Imagine teams you have been on before. Two potential scenarios may play out:

1. You can probably think of several examples of when **the goal is clear, but the commitment is low** amongst team members. Here are some possible scenarios when this phenomenon may show:

    *   Every fast-food restaurant and movie theater has a goal of customer service, but not every employee is fully committed to delivering this customer service.
    *   A wind symphony has a goal to deliver a powerful performance, but two clarinet players are busy with other things in their lives and not fully committed to making it work.
    *   A student group has a goal to get an A on a project, but they don't really want to put in the work to get the A. They set the goal because their teacher tells them they *need a goal*. They do want an A, but they're not committed to making it happen if it requires a tremendous amount of work.

2. It is also absolutely possible for team members to **have complete commitment to the goal but not really understand what the goal is.** Here are some possible scenarios where this phenomenon may be evident:

    *   A group meets frequently and passionately discusses how badly things need to change in the workplace. Nothing really moves forward, yet they continue to talk passionately about how things need to change. They're missing a clearly defined goal. They're just talking. The commitment to change is present, but they haven't set a goal to move forward with anything. They need a goal to help them focus their efforts.
    *   A band meets together to play music but doesn't really have a goal to accomplish anything. They're committed to the music, but they'll never amount to much until they start setting goals to record music, perform in public, etc.

A great goal can be a rallying cry for a struggling team. There are many great examples of a disbanded group that united under a common banner to make change happen. Ensuring that you have team focus is a great starting place when building unity for a new project, especially when you're trying to convince people to pursue a goal that may seem illogical.

Focus in Action: Walt Disney's "Dream"

One of my favorite stories about establishing focus takes place in 1935 with Walt Disney.

In 1935, Walt had an idea—which was different, game-changing and innovative. It would surely meet resistance, but he believed he could do it. He believed he *should* do it. He knew he had to get his team on board.[2]

Walt Disney Studios was nowhere near the entertainment powerhouse in 1935 like it is today. While Walt had been producing animated shorts for more than ten years, his studio had only been in existence for seven. In fact, his first studio in Kansas City had been unsuccessful financially. Walt Disney Studios was not far off. While they had successes with Silly Symphonies and Mickey Mouse, the Great Depression was taking its toll on the entertainment industry.

The stock market crash of 1929 caused the Roaring Twenties to come to a screeching halt. Fortunes were lost. Layoffs abounded. America was devastated. One in four Americans was jobless. With the high demand for employment, wages plummeted. Employers had access to hundreds of workers willing to work for very little for a chance at survival.

To make matters worse, the Dust Bowl began a year later.

The Dust Bowl, in conjunction with the Great Depression, devastated the American economy. The Homestead Act of 1862 was created to encourage settlers to move west by providing 160 acres for development to those willing to make the move. The Homestead Act was followed by the Kinkaid Act of 1904, which gave 640 acres to those willing to move to Nebraska, and the Enlarged Homestead Act of 1909, which increased the maximum allowable homestead to 320 acres in several states in central and western United States. Also during the early 1900s, a tremendous wave of immigrants poured into the United States—chasing the available land, plowing and planting as quick as they could. Within a short amount of time, more than 160,000,000 acres of land, roughly the size of Texas, were left plowed and barren. Then in 1930, a major drought struck the United States. Without crops holding down the soil, the Dust Bowl wreaked havoc.[3]

At the time, the Dust Bowl was the largest catastrophic event in US history. Of the 160,000,000 plowed acres, 35,000,000 acres were determined by the United State Agricultural Department to be useless for farming, while the remaining 125,000,000 acres were at risk. The financial failures and poor living conditions caused by the Dust Bowl resulted in 2.5 million—or 2% of the US population—abandoning their homes in New Mexico, Texas, Nebraska, Oklahoma, Colorado and Kansas and moving elsewhere. Many ended up in California.

The Dust Bowl combined with the effects of the Great Depression left the United States in a critical state. With so much of the nation without money to spend, the entertainment industry was a wreck.

The entertainment industry suffered major blows across the country. Millions struggled to afford food. Little was left over for entertainment. Vaudeville theaters and playhouses were closing. Movie theaters were shuttering their doors. At a time before TVs were common in households, people enjoyed their radios and each other's company. Walt Disney Studios was still popular, however. Their Silly Symphonies, Alice cartoons and, of course, Mickey Mouse entertained millions, but their cartoons were just shorts, fillers before a major feature or before news bulletins. The shorts were able to pay bills and provide a nice living for the families of Walt and Roy, but Walt knew that they wouldn't keep the company afloat in the future. Walt had to create another idea, an idea that would keep Disney relevant. If his little company were to remain relevant, he had to do something different.[4]

In 1934, Walt and Roy attended an award ceremony in Paris, France, to celebrate Walt's accomplishments in animation. In celebration of the event, the awards ceremony played six of Walt's shorts together, creating approximately 40 minutes of animated entertainment. The audience watched the six shorts and were left still wanting more. At that moment, Walt realized his animated medium was meant for more. He was going to show the world the future of film—but first he needed to get his animators on board with his goal: to create the world's first feature-length animated film.

He mulled over the idea for a little while. The new idea kept him up at night. He ran through the idea in his mind over and over. He felt it had merit, but he knew he would need others to catch the vision.

Still, he worried that his animators wouldn't *understand the goal*—or that they wouldn't *commit to a (goal)* venture that was potentially disastrous.

There were a million reasons why a full-length animated film should not be done at this time, but Walt knew it *could* be done. He just needed to get a team of people unified in *focusing on the goal*.

This also meant they would need to ignore the distractions.

Finally, he decided it was time to start, despite the unknown level of commitment from other stakeholders. He gathered his key animators and gave them each $0.50 to buy a quick dinner and report back to the sound stage for a special meeting. They returned curious about the special meeting. They weren't sure what to expect. Little did they know, it would be an evening they'd never forget.

When the team arrived at the soundstage, Walt stood on the stage with a single light beaming down from above. He told them he had an idea for their next project. It was a story that meant a lot to him, and he wanted to share it with his trusted key illustrators. He hoped they would catch his vision—understanding and committing to his goal—by the time the evening was finished.

For the next two hours, Walt acted out *Snow White and the Seven Dwarves*. He included all of the emotion, passion and excitement that you would expect from a master storyteller. He did all the voices; he acted out each part describing the mood, the weather and the costumes.

Walt captivated his audience. No one spoke. They watched and absorbed the message he was sending them. Their next animation would not include Mickey, Alice or any of the classic Silly Symphony characters. It would be about a girl, an evil witch, seven unlikely companions and love.

That's not all he was telling he was telling them. He was telling them that they were going to be pioneers. He was describing his vision of the future of Walt Disney Studios. Walt Disney Studios was going to be *the first to animate a feature-length film*. He needed them to understand and be committed to making this goal come true. He needed them to *focus* on the goal.

At this point, put yourself in the position of one of Walt's animators. Imagine one of your bosses approaching you with a seemingly impossible task. If you commit, it could bring failure for the entire company. It could cost you your job. You know that you definitely do not have the resources to make this work. There was no specific plan on how it would be achieved. Just a vision.

In this situation, let's say you have a willing and dedicated leader asking you to commit to accomplishing a never-accomplished goal. If you were to rate your focus on a 1–10 scale at this point, what would you rate it? The rating is important.

You may say, "Well, it depends on what I'm being asked to do." That's a fair statement. There is no right or wrong answer for where you fall. It's like taking a measurement of your water intake so far today. Sure, it would be great if you had already consumed the recommended eight glasses, but if not, no worries—there is time to improve.

As previously discussed, all team members are measurable on such a scale. Being on a scale, we slide back and forth depending on the day. We may be totally committed one day, then ready to abandon ship the next. This might sound like a risky way to run a team, but the good news is that fluidity means that members can be influenced up the scale—to greater levels of focus.

The focus scale is described in detail in Chapter 7, but keep this concept in mind as Walt continues to work with his animators in this new, extremely risky venture.

Immediately after witnessing Walt's vision, the artists knew that their current resources were not sufficient for such an endeavor. They needed more cameras. They needed a bigger crew. They needed more animators. They needed art classes. They were skilled at drawing silly, unrealistic figures, but they were being asked to animate life-like figures. In fact, the studio had yet to officially release an animation in color, yet Walt was asking that they not only do color, but that they also paint masterpiece sceneries. The cost of the project was in the hundreds of thousands of dollars, an amount that rivaled big-budget films of the time.

The animators didn't know how it was going to be done, but they understood his goal, believed it was worthy—and were committed to seeing it through. They had *focus*.

Disney's reputation of master storyteller and animator was being put to the test. Roy insisted that the film would not be financially profitable and pleaded with Walt to stay within his budget of $250,000.[5] Walt's ideas and additions caused Roy to go back to the bank six times to increase the loan. It eventually ended up at $1.5 million, more than the blockbusters *All Quiet on the Western Front* (1930) and *King Kong* (1933)—and twice as long to make.

Walt believed the movie needed to be told, unlike any film before and at nearly any cost. Walt frequently reminded Roy about the importance of what they were doing and the innovation they were creating. He kept Roy focused on the goal.

The animators also wavered at times, wondering if all of the trouble was worth it—and if this was the last Disney project the studio would create. Walt was there right along beside them to remind them. He frequently retold the story of *Snow White* to animators and staff members in hallways and meetings. He assured them this was the *future of animation* and assured them that they were prepared to move to the next step.

In short, he kept the animation team *focused on the goal*.

Many in the media referred to the project as "Disney's Folly." After two and a half years, it was finally time to see the audience reaction.

In December of 1937, *Snow White and the Seven Dwarves* premiered on the big screen. Walt was noticeably nervous about the release of his first full-length animated feature. He knew he could make people laugh with animation. That was the easy part, as animated characters were capable of doing and enduring anything he wanted them to.

But the questions remained: Could Walt Disney Studios produce an animation that made people feel fear, sadness and excitement? Could an animation make people cry?

Anyone who has seen a Pixar movie knows the answer to this is yes, but imagine a time when this general format was brand new. Would his goal prove to be the biggest flop ever—or the biggest success?

Celebrities and media personnel lined up to see the show. It was one of the most anticipated events of 1937 and came out at a time when the United States needed uplifting news to balance the constant negativity of the Great Depression, the Dust Bowl and the increasing likelihood of war in Europe. The audience entered the theater and settled down.

There was a brief introduction; then the movie began. At the opening scene, the audience let out an audible gasp at the beauty of the castle in the distance. It was unlike any animated feature they had ever seen. The rest of the movie captivated even the biggest cynics. Some scenes were so scary to children that they covered their eyes. Some children were even escorted out. The audience loved the dwarves and hissed at the witch. They sat in solemn silence during Snow White's funeral. Many shed tears. They cheered when the prince arrived and carried Snow White home.

Snow White was an engaging experience that changed the world. It all started with Walt Disney, on a sound stage, late in the evening, telling a story about a princess, an evil queen, seven unlikely companions and love. With this story, Walt focused more than 600 staff members on a crazy goal—so much so that they willingly worked long hours for low pay to bring to pass an incredible story.

Focus is a powerful tool in accomplishing great tasks—and contributing to team unity.

Shifting Priorities, Shifting Focus

Focus is also a common reason for groups to break up. People's goals change. It can be caused by a situational change, such as COVID-19, or a personal change, such as realizing you don't want what you thought you wanted. This is common in the entertainment industry. Many new actors join acting guilds and sign up with talent agents in hopes of being discovered as the next big star, but for most people, acting is a lot of hard work. It requires lots of rejection and constant networking. It's common for a group of friends to move to New York in hopes of pursuing their dreams—working together to fully commit to a goal—then they discover the goal isn't exactly what they thought they wanted. One by one, they break up and abandon the dream. This happens with bands, too. This is extremely common in relationships. Focus can keep people together. It can also break people apart.

Sometimes team members can be extremely focused at first, then have other priorities that take greater precedence. This waning of focus happens frequently with music groups.

One Direction: Shared Focus for Short-Term Success

The meteoric success of the group One Direction is nearly unfathomable. In 2010, five young men—Niall, Harry, Liam, Louis and Zayne—tried out for the X Factor. All five were cut from the boot camp stage. They had made it past the initial rounds of a major competition which made such participants as Olly Murs, Leona Lewis and JLS major stars. Many others have continued their music careers with their publicity boosts from The X Factor.[6]

Niall, Harry, Liam, Louis and Zayn all shared similar stories. Their parents all mentioned their love for singing and performing. The only thing Niall loved as much as singing and performing was soccer. Zayne and Louis had already written songs. Harry performed whenever he had the chance. Liam, while shy, still never missed an opportunity to hold the mic. Given their passion and commitment to music, it came as a major blow to all five of these young men to be cut from the show so close to the live show.[7]

Then something unprecedented changed their lives forever.

The young men received phone calls. Simon Cowell and others believed that these young men deserved another shot but not as a solo act. They were provided an opportunity to make it to the X Factor live rounds if they performed in a group with four other young men who were cut in the same round. Each agreed, willing to take a chance on this strange opportunity.

The first time One Direction officially met as a group was at Harry's house. They ate, swam and talked. They just enjoyed being together. None of them knew what to expect or how successful they were going to be. They were just having a good time. It was there that they decided to give it their all. They decided to not be a "typical" boy band with choreographed moves performed to sweet harmonies. They were going to do it their way and have a good time doing it.

This first meeting at Harry's house was critical. All five mentioned it in their autobiography as an important time in setting the stage for One Direction. Their goal was to be different from previous boy bands. They weren't going to learn dances. They weren't going to perform in unison and wear the same clothes. If they were going to do this, they were going to do it their way—and have fun.[8]

They committed to these goals. These goals were their guiding lights during the first few years of their time together. They established their focus.

Their popularity spread worldwide with their release "What Makes You Beautiful." The song released in September 2011 and became a worldwide hit, quickly becoming Sony Music's number one most pre-ordered song in history. The rest of the album was released in December 2011 and hit the charts in the top 10 in over 30 countries, debuting at number one in the United Kingdom.

Once the album was recorded, they headed to the United States to promote it and their upcoming tour. The big announcement about their tour was made on *The Today Show*. The band was blown away by their reception.[9]

Up to this point, the band was focused on having a good time making music. They were enjoying their new life with their new careers. Harry, Niall, Louis, Liam and Zayne all mentioned how much they missed their families and friends. They all mentioned how much they looked forward to contributing more to the creation of the music for their next album, but all in all, they were having a great time performing and touring—and were very grateful for their time together.

By the time the third album was released in 2013, the band was a world phenomenon. One Direction was filling stadiums around the world. They were meeting celebrities and being provided opportunities to collaborate on music projects independent from One Direction. They went to exclusive parties and explored their lives as talented artists. At this point, their focus changed. Their goal to continue performing as a group began to shift. Playing as a group was fun, but they were each building their own media careers, making connections with other artists and producers. Each of them was working on their own music, and most of them were getting tired of the constant travel. They missed their family, friends and freedom—freedom to manage their own schedules and freedom to create their own music. Their focus was shifting from their group's success to their success beyond One Direction.

In 2014, Zayne began to publicly mention that he wasn't the biggest fan of the music they were creating and that while he was pleased with the increased participation in creating the third album, he wanted to explore other music.[10] He also increasingly missed his family. The group would be away from home almost 75% of the year, leaving about 90 days spread between a tight schedule to visit with family and friends. The life of a bandmate was wearing thin.[11] Other members of One Direction felt the same, though it was Zayne that made the first move. In 2015, Zayne left the group. By 2016, despite the extremely successful release of their first album without Zayne, they decided to part ways; the band broke up.

What had started as a young, fun group of boys looking to have a good time turned into a group of men looking to chart their own courses in the world of music. The breakup wasn't necessarily a poor decision. The goals of the group had changed. They looked to pursue their own careers as artists. They had met their initial goals to have fun and see the world, but as the group learned and developed, they moved on. Their focus shifted from band success to individual success. Since then, each former One Direction member has had successful solo releases.

Refocusing After Disaster

Focus can also help a group heal from disaster. The strength of focus required in times of crises can even help a team build unity more quickly and strongly than they would during "easy" times.

In Louisville, Kentucky, a small theater group was reeling from a major catastrophe caused by an ousted leader. He had been voted out because of unethical behavior with other actors and finances. When he left, a group followed him out the door. Those who stayed behind were disengaged and fearful. The actors and administrators weren't sure how to continue. Their funds were depleted, and their reputation was tarnished. Attendance had dramatically dropped. Fear, distrust and uncertainty were commonly felt among the employees, patrons, actors and donors.[12]

A new leader was hired. He was aware of what had happened. He was aware of the dysfunction that existed—but not of its magnitude.

While many might shirk away from such a potentially disastrous position, he actively sought it out. He was a successful person and could easily find other work, but he wanted this position because he believed in the organization and its potential. He just needed to help refocus the stakeholders toward the future.

To do this he followed the guidance of Michael Kaiser in his excellent book titled *The Art of the Turnaround*.

His first act was to shift everyone to look at the future. When he started, the group was focused on the past. The group members wanted to make sure the new director knew what had happened and what the previous administration had done.

While there is merit to focusing on the past to understand what went wrong, he felt his team was too focused on these traumas to promote future growth and healing. Instead, he subtly and progressively replaced their rhetoric with positive visions of the future.

In his first few meetings with his team, it seemed half of the meeting would be spent discussing the past. He could see that they were hurt by the recent actions. He acknowledged their hurt, but would follow it up with, "Let me show you what I've been thinking. . . ." He shared about his positive conversations with community members and donors. His point was to show them that while the past hurt, their future was still bright. There was hope. They still had fans. They just needed to stay focused in the turnaround. He needed them to let go and commit to improving their situation.

In following the plan, the next assignment was to hire a new crew to replace the half of the crew who had abruptly left. He held brief interviews in which he asked the candidates to give their impression of the future of the company. He would then share his vision for the future.

As he shared, he would watch for signs of excitement and a willingness to jump in. He was up front about the challenges that lay ahead, but he would assure his candidates that if they were willing to help, they would have success. When his new crew joined his motivated current crew, success soon followed.

Over the next few years, the theater troupe saw a steady increase in attendance and donations. The marketing team developed new materials and highlighted the successes. The leadership team diversified the offerings to include different shows to energize the local residents. They made deals with food trucks and vendors to allow people to make an evening of it, grabbing a dinner or snack and enjoying the show.

With these changes and many others, 2019 was their highest year yet, breaking records on attendance, sponsorships and overall income. Their reputation had rebounded, and actors from around the area looked to join this group.

The journey was long and required many late nights and difficult decisions. It required constant reminders and refocusing of priorities and goals—where they were headed and how far they had traveled on their new path—but it all started with a director getting a group of people committed to delivering a great show.

Rolling the Dice: An Exercise in Commitment

I've shared grand-scale, amazing examples of the importance of focus. Here's a smaller example. I love teaching, training, coaching and anything else that helps people learn and grow. I'm in fact extremely passionate about it. One thing I have learned is sometimes it's difficult to demonstrate the importance of what I am teaching to a group of college students. To help explain concepts, I utilize *experiential learning theory*.[13] The idea is to create an opportunity for students to *experience* the concept I'm trying to get across. By tapping into their first-hand experience with an exercise related to the concepts I'm teaching, understanding and retention are dramatically increased.

When I needed students to understand that the importance of focusing is more than just setting a goal, I created an activity that I have since used several times with very similar results.

First, I hand each student a six-sided die. These are normal dice purchased at my local game shop. With normal six-sided dice, the odds of rolling a six are one in six. I tell students I will time them for one minute. Their job is to roll as many sixes as possible.

Super simple, right? I give them a moment to ask questions.

The most common is, "So, just roll the die? That's it?"

"Yes. Just roll the die. Count how many times you roll a six. That's it."

The students sit up straight. I say, "Roll," and the rolling commences.

They roll as many times as they can until the 60 seconds passed. Then they add up how many sixes they rolled and reported back.

One by one, I ask for their scores and write them down on the whiteboard. The students who rolled more than 10 sixes proudly announce their scores. The ones that rolled four or fewer sheepishly announce their scores.

The class average is normally around 6.2 sixes rolled per person.

I then ask how many sixes they feel like they *can* actually roll in one minute. I'm usually met with silence—though there are always a few that shout out absurdities: "100!" "1,000!" (I keep my classes rather informal. I'm glad they feel comfortable enough to joke like that.)

After a few seconds, more serious responses start to trickle out. "Eight?" "Maybe nine?"

I then respond with a high number, normally 15 to 20. This is to demonstrate how ineffective goals are that are perceived as much too high to reach. I tell them that I really want them to reach that number and to try their best to reach it. Students are in disbelief. They have zero confidence that they can reach such a high number, but they get ready to roll anyway. The time starts; the rolling begins.

At the end of this minute, the students count up their scores and start reporting. Again, the ones that get above a ten are so proud of their accomplishment that they actually start to almost scoff at other people that have yet to get above a ten. Most students roll around six or seven sixes, while a few are still at four or less. The average the second time is normally around 6.7.

By this point, they are fairly convinced that reaching anything much higher is near impossible. "Dr. Ross, this is a game of chance. There's nothing we can do."

Isn't there? Is there really *nothing* you can do?

I express my sincere desire that they reach 12. They scoff. They just had two trials and haven't yielded anything higher than a seven, so why would they believe that they could accomplish anything better?

I get it. We often encounter this phenomenon. People have never seen anything better, so it must not exist, right?

Well, that's not the only thing at play here. It's not just that they haven't seen anything better; it's that they're not quite sure how to get there. They're trying their hardest, but they're still not realizing the results that they want to get, so they come up with excuses. *It's just a game of chance, so why commit?*

It's interesting to note at this point that most individuals in the group have confidence in themselves, but they don't have confidence in the rest of the group. This is a very common feeling I hear when I work with teams. *If everyone were like me, then we'd be great!* As rude as this may sound, they're right. And the person next to them who also thinks everyone should be like him/her is also right. *Everyone* thinking that is right: Everyone needs to be focused together to reach the goal.

I assure the class that it can, in fact, be done. I point out that there are people in the class that have successfully rolled ten-plus sixes each time that we've done it. *Maybe they know something.* I instill a little *hope*; then I step back and let them talk.

One student says, "Well, what do you all do?"

The first response is normally, "I just roll the die." Well, yes, that is what that person did, but as they discuss further, they start to realize there are differences in how everyone is rolling. Rolling on a desk causes the die to bounce for several seconds before slowing down, reducing the amount of rolling you can do. Rolling on a notebook eliminates the bounce. Also, it is normally pointed out that keeping track of your score in your head is a lot faster than rolling a six, picking up your pencil, then rolling again. Normally someone also points out that people are actually shaking the die in their hand for a full second or two just to roll the die. All that's needed is a quick pick-up and flip in order to re-roll the die. Armed with these tips and tricks, they are ready to try again, feeling much more confident that they can meet their goal.

The time starts, and the rolling begins.

The room is much quieter as everyone is focused. People aren't dropping dice or checking their phones anymore. They're not laughing or looking at anyone else's rolling. They're all staring straight at their dice. Some are lying on the floor. Some are still at their desks. Some are rolling on a notebook in their laps. They've all improved their situation and rolled. When the minute is complete, the class is filled with smiling faces.

This time, nearly every person in the class rolled ten-plus sixes. The lowest average I have had after the final attempt is 11.5. I've had many score much higher than 12.

What lesson does this teach us? When the students thought that the task was pointless, they put forth low effort. They knew the goal, and even *understood* the goal, but they weren't *committed to* achieving it. Many felt it was impossible or pointless, so why try?

Of course, there are other components at work, but once they committed as a group to roll 12 sixes in one minute, they began putting forth effort to figure it out. They put down their other distractions and focused and committed on working together the best they could to accomplish their goal of doubling their output.

Setting a goal and gaining commitment to establish focus is a powerful first step in building team unity.

Notes

1. Bird, L., & MacMullan, J. (1999). *Bird watching: On playing and coaching the game I love.* Warner Books.
2. Samels, M. (2017, August 29). *The American experience: Walt Disney.* PBS.
3. Duncan, D., Duncan, D., Burns, K., & Dunfey, J. (2012). *The dust bowl: A film by Ken Burns [DVD].* PBS.
4. Samels, M. (2017, August 29). *The American experience: Walt Disney.* PBS.
5. Snow White and the Seven Dwarfs. (2005, September 16). Disney Wiki. https://disney.fandom.com/wiki/Snow_White_and_the_Seven_Dwarfs
6. Direction, O. (2013). *1D: Where we are: Our band, our story.* Harper, an imprint of HarperCollins Publishers.
7. Direction, O. (2014). *Who we are: Our official autobiography.* HarperCollins Publishers.
8. Direction, O. (2014). *Who we are: Our official autobiography.* HarperCollins Publishers.
9. Direction, O. (2013). *1D: Where we are: Our band, our story.* Harper, an imprint of HarperCollins Publishers.
10. Dambrosio, C., & DiFiore, P. (2021, July 23). From throwing insults to talking about a reunion, here's everything one direction members have said since their hiatus. Insider. www.insider.com/everything-one-direction-has-said-about-each-other-since-breakup-2019–5#one-direction-has-been-on-hiatus-since-2015–1
11. Direction, O. (2014). *Who we are: Our official autobiography.* HarperCollins Publishers.
12. Ross, J. (2020, May 18). Kentucky Shakespeare Recovery. personal.
13. Kolb, D. A. (2014). *Experiential learning: Experience as the source of learning and development.* FT Press.

Chapter 4

Unity Component #2—Direction

It has been well established that teams need goals to reach peak performance, but rarely is *direction* discussed. Direction is crucial because in business, it's not necessarily the resources we have but how we use them. As famed motivational speaker and self-help guru Zig Ziglar states:

> *Lack of direction, not lack of time, is the problem. We all have 24-hour days.*
>
> —*Zig Ziglar*

No matter how great your goal is, it will be very difficult to experience success without solid direction. Direction, as it pertains to team unity, is a plan or strategy for how you will get to your goal.

Just like focus, direction is broken up into two parts: *understanding the plan* and *committing to the plan*.

Similar to focus, there also are several scenarios in which a person can understand the plan and not be committed to it:

- In a meeting, when the team commits to a goal but the leader lays out a plan (way of achieving that goal) that many disagree with
- Parents who are helping their children earn good grades by encouraging the sacrifice of screen time in exchange for an increase in study time. The child could be totally committed to achieving the goal but disagree that cutting screen time is the way to get there.
- When simply following a recipe for "The Best Chocolate Chip Cookies," someone disagrees with the amount of chocolate chips required for the recipe (instead wanting to add more chips and mix half dark and half semi-sweet).

There are also several scenarios when a person may be committed to the plan but not really understand the plan.

DOI: 10.4324/9781003269038-7

- Famed Muppet creator Jim Henson assigned his New York team to work on *The Dark Crystal*, then left for London, where he would do much of his filming. The team worked hard, fully committed to the plan he laid out, but they ran into issues when much of what they were doing was innovative and needed his expertise. They would then be forced to pause to wait for his expertise.[1]
- A student works on a group project for hours, fully committed and dedicated to the goal and the plan, only to find out she was working on the wrong part of the project (true story).
- What many "checking-the-box" leaders do: They walk around, doing what a clever speaker or book told them to do, so they can "check the box" and sleep better at night—knowing that they were *a better leader today*. While they're committed to the plan and goal, they don't understand that they need to care about their employees and help them do the same.

Understanding and committing to a goal are very different from understanding and committing to a plan. That's the point of the direction component when it comes to the scale and The Unity Formula; you will learn to measure a team's understanding and commitment to the plan.

When my wife and I were first married, I bought her a curio cabinet for a few collectibles she had. It was a large and beautiful wood cabinet with beautiful glass and lights. Assembly was required. I was young and didn't have much experience putting things together, but I could do this. No problem, right?

The first step in the instructions was "Two People Required for Proper Assembly." It was capitalized, bolded, and everything. I read it and did what many of you have done . . . ignored it. More than two hours later, I was still working on the cabinet, ready it throw it through my front window. Instructions, the plans for assembly, are important.

Now imagine a team of people working together. They're committed to traveling toward a destination. They see the reason why everyone should do anything to get there. As they start their travels, other potential opportunities arise. Every path may seem to lead to the same destination, but getting to the same place is not a sure thing—nor is traveling together. Everyone is committed to the destination, but if no one is committed to the direction they should travel, then eventually everyone may end up on a separate path, all alone.

If you've ever seen a horror movie, you've seen this play out time and time again. "Don't go alone!" is what you want to scream. No one actually wants to see a scary movie where everyone escapes on their first try; however, we keep watching even when they go alone into that shed with all the chainsaws and dark corners. Saying to their extremely strong friend who is trained in martial arts, "Hey, buddy, I have to head out to this creepy shed, and I think it would be great if you came with me for protection" would just not set the stage for a scary scene.

You can look at tackling your goal as if you're building a project or traveling on a journey. Either way, even if you start with focusing on the best goal in the world, you won't go very far unless you head in the same direction as the rest of the team—united and committed to following the plan.

Everyone Knows and Fulfills Their Roles

Team members with a high level of direction are dedicated to the strategy of accomplishing the goal and committed to fulfilling their role. If everyone agrees with the strategy and fulfills their role in that strategy, then we see a tremendous amount of success. If just one member of the group decides to follow a different strategy, then success can wane.

Here's a brief example of an author demonstrating the importance of working together on a single strategy.

More than 60 years ago, a young English teacher had an idea for a book. I will share the interesting backstory and then the tie-in to direction as it pertains to unity. . . . This author had always wanted to write a book. Since the age of 12, he had made several literary attempts, but this was his first attempt to actively pursue publication.

More than 20 publishers rejected his manuscript. Publishers didn't see a point in publishing such a negative work or felt that the story really didn't have a plot. A group of boys get trapped on an island, chaos ensues, then it is quickly and suddenly resolved. The protagonist is weak and does not grow or overcome evil. Instead, evil wins. Surely this book would not appeal to a broader audience.

Eventually, one publisher saw the merit in publishing such a book. After a few revisions and correspondence, William Golding's book *Lord of the Flies* was eventually published in 1954.[2]

Lord of the Flies is a book about the difference in direction. Ralph was the selected leader. He was small but mature and could think clearly about setting a path forward that would lead to survival. He organized the camp into groups and established a hunting party, a gathering party, a signal fire and a form of government. His plan was to *work together methodically to reach the goal of survival until rescue.* Everyone seemed mostly on board with the direction, until the situation changed.

A potential danger arrived on the island. The "littleuns" had terrible dreams of monsters in the dark. Ralph's established direction would lead them to survival until rescue, but it did not provide protection from island monsters. Jack proposed a new direction. His new direction addressed the more immediate danger of the monster on the island. Everyone on the island wanted to survive. But Jack's group, encouraged by the success of its hunting trip, believed Jack was more capable of leading the group to safety by protecting the group from the more immediate danger of the island monster. The boys eventually joined Jack.

Jack's ways became savage. He promoted strength and punished the weak. His followers believed, as Jack did, that the weak were holding them back from achieving their full potential. His actions led to the death of many boys who stood in the way of the strong.

Lord of the Flies did end up appealing to a broader audience. The success of the book lead Sir William Golding to write 11 more novels, but none received as much success as *Lord of the Flies*. Its appeal is still prevalent today with many business and culture sites such as *Times*, *Business Insider* and *Inc.* recently posting articles about preventing a *Lord of the Flies* scenario in the workplace. Indeed, there seems to be a prevalent idea that if people are left unattended then everyone will split into factions, each with its own strategies. Then a riotous frenzy will break out, the workplace will be set ablaze and profits will plummet. . . .

But it doesn't have to be that way. It's very possible to both empower people to move forward while keeping the team focused on the overall strategy.

Conducting and Cascading Direction Without a Leader

Common orchestra structure, whether formal or informal, is to have a conductor and section leaders. The conductor works with the section leaders to ensure that the members play the parts appropriately. The section leaders then work with the individual members to help them master their music pieces before the big performance.

Many professional orchestras have moved beyond the need for section leaders, as instrument mastery and professionalism are requirements for a position in the orchestra—but the conductor remains in almost every orchestra around the world. In fact, in some orchestras the conductor is the main attraction, with his or her face displayed prominently on fliers and billboards throughout the city.

It makes sense, right? After all, it is the conductor who helps establish focus and direction for the members and holds them accountable for performance. The conductor also helps with marketing, booking performances, finances, hiring new performers, scheduling and much more. In other words, the conductor helps ensure the direction of each person involved is focused on the same overall strategy.

Truly, conductors play a very important part in orchestra success, but what if you didn't have a conductor?

Instead of hearing the collective ideas and interpretations of the group, many orchestras only play what the conductor would like them to play—and how the conductor believes they should play. In 1972, a group of performers decided that they were all professional performing artists and that all of their ideas should be heard. Orpheus Chamber Orchestra in New York City chose not to have a conductor. In their opinion, a conductor, while very useful, could also restrict the creativity of the group.[3]

As you may have guessed based on the context of how I set up the story, this story ends well—but not until after some hard work was done.

Initially, the group started off strong, as the founders all believed in the idea and concept; but without a clear leader, the disagreements started fairly quickly. *When is practice? What do we perform? Where are we performing? How are we going to pay for this? How are we going to advertise?* These questions and more needed to be addressed quickly before the orchestra moved forward. They needed a plan—a strategy—on how they were going to setup this creative chamber orchestra.

So, they communicated. They shared their strengths, weaknesses and limitations. They discussed what needed to be done. The chamber members were committed to the plan. So committed, in fact, that people volunteered to take over different roles in order to contribute to the overall success of the group. Members continued helping the orchestra be successful and established a set of rules and guidelines to establish the overall direction.[4]

In other words, they understood and were committed to the *goal* of being a great, creative and conductor-less chamber orchestra (focus)—and understood and were committed to developing and executing a *plan* or *strategy* to ensure success (direction).

Today, the Grammy award–winning orchestra routinely performs at Carnegie Hall and has over 70 albums. They continue to perform around the world and have even started an educational program to reach out to youth interested in music. They continue to struggle at times, as would any group of people, but they follow a set of guidelines and procedures for communicating. They still have gossiping and other concerns that other groups would have, but the difference is they have agreed on how to move forward. When faced with a new threat, they meet again and together decide what the new direction should be.[5]

You might be thinking, "Yeah, but these people were not stuck on an island like in *Lord of the Flies*. They had a way out of the orchestra if they wanted to. Besides, they were professionals." Okay, yes, that is true. Over their 50 years of history, performers have disagreed with the direction of the Orpheus Chamber Orchestra and even left the orchestra to pursue their own paths, but the point is they worked together without a leader forcing them to do so. The ones who stayed chose to stay because they had high levels of focus and direction.

An Internship in Building Direction

Alright, here's another example of a group of interns who had the same goal *and* who, like the orchestra, chose to work together on a common strategy for success.

In the summer of 2004, a group of approximately ten interns at one of the world's top manufacturing facilities gathered together on a project. This group consisted of engineers and supply chain majors from some of the top universities in the country. It was truly a talented and motivated team, with members having worked on a wide variety of projects with impressive results. Additionally, internships at this organization frequently led to job offers. This was a very recognizable Fortune 100 company that may not have been on the top of everyone's future employment list but would have been an excellent resume addition no matter where any of the interns decided to work next. The internship provided tremendous incentive to work and excel.

Their task was presented to them. They were then dismissed to start their work.

There was one major problem. No one knew what to do next. They didn't know who to talk to, where to get their resources or how to evaluate their success. No leader had been named. They were all just interns in a facility with thousands of employees.[6]

For the next ten weeks, this project was to be their number one priority. The immediate response was not a flurry of excitement for their big opportunity. The interns were frustrated. They were motivated to complete the goal. They were committed to making it a tremendous success, but the lack of resources depleted morale.

For the first two days, the interns continued with their other priorities. They gossiped about the managers and the company—how the company had brought them on as interns, then abandoned them. Some even expressed so much discontent with the company that they mentioned not wanting to work with a company as disorganized as this one.

They also met with other interns from around the company and heard many positive stories about active managers involved with the day-to-day tasks of the interns, along with lunch meetings and introductions of top leadership. This made matters worse. They thought that everyone else would get ahead of them because their managers were helping their projects.

This team felt discouraged. They didn't know what to do, but they knew they still didn't want the ten weeks to be a failure, even if they didn't plan on working at this company in the future.

They were achievers. While a few of their fellow interns in other areas faced similar scenarios and decided they would only work as hard as they were forced to work, this group of interns wanted more. They wanted to stay active in their work. They met together and talked about how great it would be to really figure out this project and excel. It was a great company with great pay and benefits. Doing well at this project would almost guarantee them a position. They committed to figuring out the project.

By the third day, the interns began asking leaders, supervisors and more experienced employees around them for advice. They were timid. Everyone else seemed so busy compared with them—with their full-time jobs and meetings. Some were rarely at their desks.

"Ultimately, everyone was great," an intern explained in a conversation with me. "[Management] liked seeing a group of interns trying to be successful. They gave us all the time they could, which was great, because we knew absolutely nothing. Nothing at all. We would visit with one employee, then have to go back and look up the acronyms and words they had just told us, but we were too afraid to ask. It was crazy but good times. We felt like investigators trying to sort through a puzzle."

After a few weeks, the interns found themselves in meetings with senior leadership, making connections with key individuals. They realized that the project they were assigned was short-sighted. In order to truly make a difference, they would have to take the project much further, reaching all the way out to the supplier and the customer.

"The project we were assigned was just a small project for interns," stated the intern in our interview. "They didn't expect much from us. They just wanted us to lay the groundwork for them to take over, but we had done so much and had so much time left over, we asked if we could continue. There was so much more work, and we didn't have anything better to do; plus, this became *our* project. We were having a blast. We'd hang out outside of work and talk about it, and ride together to work, then work all day together. Such a good time."

By week seven, their project had far exceeded the expectations of their superiors. This group of interns, all strangers at the start of the project, were now spending nearly all of their time together at work and after work. Their success caught the attention of many influential people in the company. In week nine, the group of interns not only presented their project to a senior leadership team including the vice president, but they also presented a list of future work that needed to be accomplished to see the project through. These interns were clear on a direction and committed to it; they had in fact created it, with help from those around them.

The result? All of the interns in this group were hired. In fact, the one interviewed for the story was hired into their leadership development program and sent to the UK to continue on the project he started as an intern.

I am in no way suggesting that we provide interns with very little guidance so they can "figure it out." This can be very demoralizing and can cause a decrease in commitment to the goal by diminishing hope in success. In this case, however, their lack of guidance started as a major hurdle but turned out to be a major strength to their success. Because they didn't know what to do, they had to work together to evaluate all of their options every step of the way and develop their own path forward. Because they created it together, they were committed to the steps toward goal completion. Communication and evaluation were constant. There were many missteps. They discovered many dead ends. Many of the employees the interns spoke with, including senior leadership, provided advice and suggestions that ended up not working out. But the interns' determination to be successful and relentless, hopeful attitudes propelled them forward—searching for other ways to accomplish their goal. Their adoption and belief in not only their goal but also in their plan to reach their goal (direction) led to their success.

Direction, once we get to discussing the unity scale and The Unity Formula, represents how dedicated people are to the plan to accomplish the goal. A plan like the one we just visited in the intern story tends to have a more solid long-term direction with a very fluid short term. The interns knew their goal, but they weren't sure how to get there. As they learned more about the process and why overcoming the problem would benefit the company, they discovered steps that would help lead them toward their goal. Some steps led to dead ends, but the point is they decided to try something new together.

Define and Know Roles and Boundaries

Another important note about direction is the importance of everyone knowing the boundaries of their tasks and roles. It is incredibly demoralizing to discover that you are duplicating the work of someone else. Repeating work is inefficient and a quick way for an employee to feel unimportant, which leads to a host of other organizational behavior problems. In some cases, duplication of efforts can also cause a major breakdown in team performance, such as in basketball.

Basketball is a great example of teamwork. It's fast-paced and requires quick adjustments, hard work and trust in the coaching and other players. With only five people on the court at a time from your team, every member must be fully engaged. A defense will quickly be mitigated, or an offense will shut down, if players do not know and understand their roles in the plays.

Coach Phil Jackson was known for winning: 11 championship rings as a coach. Two as a player. Thirteen rings in total. He coached the Bulls through six championships, then the Lakers for five more. Michael Jordan, Scottie Pippen, Dennis Rodman, Kobe Bryant and Shaquille O'Neill were just a few of his all-stars over the years. Many would say that with this caliber of talent, of course he would have rings. But talent doesn't win championships. Teamwork does, which is why Phil Jackson is the first to admit one of the key contributors to his success was the triangle offense.

There are many offenses and defenses in the NBA. Some are simple—utilizing a few players and key plays—while others are more difficult to implement, but the triangle offense is arguably the most difficult to implement, with a few players even mentioning that a degree in basketball science was required for proper implementation. The implementation of the triangle offense, as with other offenses, requires all five players to constantly be aware of the locations of the ball and the defense. It tends to be a reactionary offense. No plays required. Just look at what the defense is doing and adjust accordingly. It would take months for a player to full grasp the complexities of the offense, but when it worked, it maintained spacing on the court and would leave an open scorer nearly every time.

There's a lot of debate surrounding the effectiveness of the triangle offense in today's NBA. Bringing up the triangle offense is in no way intended to debate its effectiveness compared with other of the more common offenses today. I also recognize that many have made the claim that the offense was so successful because they had some of the NBA's most talented players using the offense. How could it not work? I understand, and I get that argument.

The point isn't about the effectiveness of the offense but rather this: In order to maintain a high level of direction, everyone needs to be fully engaged in their specific role for it to work at maximum efficiency. In this case, the players needed to be engaged in their role in the offense. Michael Jordan was quick to recognize its potential and pushed his teammates to follow the plan.

The late Kobe Bryant, on the other hand, was less patient. He was guilty on many occasions of ignoring the triangle offense—and thus lowering the unity of the team.[7]

Kobe didn't lack talent or focus. But focus alone—without unified direction—is not enough to achieve team unity. Could Kobe join the Lakers' direction?

He was raised by a former NBA player who married the daughter of another NBA player. From the age of three, Kobe showed an extreme interest in the sport. In a very short time, he dominated the game as a junior high player in Italy. In eighth grade, the family moved to Philadelphia, where he continued to excel in every way. In high school, he played every position. His drive and extreme competitive spirit were unrivaled.

He was good, but that wasn't good enough. His goal was to be great—so that remained his focus.

His senior year of high school, Kobe had already acquired a long list of honors, including Naismith High School Player of the Year, Gatorade Men's National Basketball Player of the Year, a first-team Parade

All-American and a *USA Today* All-USA First Team player. Colleges actively recruited Kobe with promises of playing time and NBA scout recognition, but Kobe wasn't interested. The hype and attention around Kevin Garnett's straight-out-of-high-school entry into the NBA interested Kobe. He opted to skip college and enter the 1996 NBA draft. With his incredible offensive and defensive statistics and his maturity and intelligence, he quickly became one of the most anticipated recruits in the draft. With a little bit of maneuvering, the Lakers acquired Kobe with a three-year, $3.5 million deal.

With hard work and determination, Kobe quickly stepped up to the heightened NBA challenge. By his third year, he was starting for the Lakers, but he still failed to deliver a championship ring despite three playoff appearances. Laker fans demanded more. Phil Jackson received a phone call.

Phil entered his new coaching position in the 1999–2000 year. Phil brought with him Tex Winter and The Triangle Offense. Phil and Tex immediately went to work implementing the offense in practices. Kobe was a tremendous scorer and thoroughly enjoyed one-on-one offensive bouts, which, as a shooting guard, was in his purview, but such independent work ignores the rest of his very capable team. He adopted the triangle offense (the team's direction, in the form of a strategy or plan) but needed to be reminded at times not to resort back to his aggressive Kobe-centered style of play. He was great, and he knew it, but the triangle offense required that everyone play their part, or it didn't work. In his book *11 Rings*, Jackson reminisced on a few times that Kobe abandoned the plan, resorting back to his old style of Kobe-centered, little-teamwork-required style of play—causing the team's offense (and unity) to fall apart.

Most of the time, his reverting to a more selfish style of play occurred when his team was losing or when he felt other players weren't performing at the level Kobe believed they needed. One of his most frequent targets was all-star and seasoned MVP Shaquille O'Neil.

Kobe's selfish playing frustrated his teammates, as they felt more like observers instead of participants in the offense. Part of this was because the triangle offense frequently utilized Shaq's dominance at center, providing him the opportunities Kobe desired to have. This led to many heated arguments at practice (compromising unity, as we will discuss in the component of conflict), which eventually spilled out in public.

During these early days of the triangle offense, Kobe thought that the team should center offensive efforts on his playing strengths instead of on Shaq. Phil felt differently. He would tell Kobe to "trust the triangle" and "wait for the game to come to you—be patient." With Kobe taking over the direction, the team was left less unified, feeling less a part of the success and leading to an increase in frustration.

The frustration took a toll on team performance.

Teams high in direction know their role. They know where to go and what is expected of them. If they encounter any problems, they get assistance. When they encounter a unique challenge, they adjust—as a team pivoting into a new path that they believe will lead to the next score. If that path doesn't work, they adjust again, but the point is, no one person is the scorer. They are all working together, each with a role that will contribute to the overall success of the project.

Teams that are low in direction tend to have multiple people attempting to do the same job. They have people attempting to be *the* key point provider, or they lack the organization and agility to handle a project's inconveniences that inevitably pop up along the way. In other words, similar to the Bulls and Lakers mastering the triangle offense, those high in direction not only know their role but also understand that their role may change depending on the situation, and they are okay with that. They are committed to doing their part and doing it well. Similar to when a player would try to dominate the triangle offense, the team might still get a goal in the short term, but the long-term performance of the team suffers.

It's safe to say that not only did Kobe expertly execute the triangle but also that he learned to love the triangle. During his first three championships, he needed to be reminded to play team basketball. By the 2008–2009 season, he was encouraging his fellow teammates to play the triangle offense, assisting with the coaching and team unity. In fact, in 2015, one year before his retirement, Kobe was noted several times for criticizing the Knicks' poorly executed "triangle offense,[8]" highlighting the benefits of the triangle when executed properly and making sure to point out the poor execution of the Knicks' attempt at the triangle. In 2017, Kobe mentioned that he was using the triangle offense to coach his daughter's team with great success.[9] His direction became clearer, as executing it became more routine. This heightened commitment and passion for the direction in turn deepened the team's unity.

Focus is the commitment to the goal. Direction is the commitment to the plan. While they share many similarities, they are distinct characteristics of a unified team.

Notes

1. Jones, B. J. (2016). *Jim Henson: The biography*. Ballantine Books.
2. Biography.com Editors. (2021, May 26). William Golding. Biography.com. www.biography.com/writer/william-golding
3. Orpheus Chamber Orchestra. (n.d.). About us. Orpheus Chamber Orchestra. https://orpheusnyc.org/about/about-us.
4. EuroArts Music International. (2005). Orpheus Chamber Orchestra Presents: Music Meets Business. Germany. www.youtube.com/watch?v=HtblP6ECnbI

5. Orpheus Chamber Orchestra. (n.d.). About us. Orpheus Chamber Orchestra. https://orpheusnyc.org/about/about-us

6. Ross, J. (2013, March 22). Josh's Internship. personal.

7. Jackson, P., & Delehanty, H. (2014). *Eleven rings: The soul of success*. Penguin Press.

8. The PostGame Staff. (2015, November 9). Kobe on knicks: 'ain't no f***in' triangle'. ThePostGame.com. www.thepostgame.com/dish/201511/kobe-bryant-spike-lee-new-york-knicks-triangle-offense-los-angeles-lakers-carmelo

9. Medworth, W. (2017, December 8). Kobe Bryant is running the triangle offense with his daughter's basketball team. SBNation.com. www.sbnation.com/nba/2017/12/8/16753426/kobe-bryant-triangle-offense-daughters-basketball-team

Research Note: Focus and Direction = Hope

Just a brief pause from the discussion about the four components of unity to briefly mention a critical occurrence that happens naturally as a team increases their focus and direction. Focus and direction are extremely powerful because together they create hope.

When a team is fully committed to goals and to the plan to accomplish the goals, they have hope. The hope discussed here is not just wishful thinking like "I hope it doesn't rain today" or "I hope no one noticed that I ripped my pants during that demonstration" (true story). Hope is a vital component in goal accomplishment.

Hope is one of four components of psychological capital, a set of internal resources that helps us buffer the demands of work. In other words, when the demands of work are high, these four components help repel the negative emotional consequences that can occur. The four components are hope, efficacy, resilience and optimism (HERO).[1] Hope is the belief that a chosen pathway will lead to goal accomplishment, self-efficacy refers to a person's trust in their abilities to accomplish goals, resilience is the ability to rebound from tough times and optimism is an overall positive outlook on life. Of these four, hope is the most powerful.[2]

Hope is "a cognitive set that is based on a reciprocally derived sense of successful (a) willpower (fortitude and capability to pursue a goal) and (b) waypower (a path to accomplish the goal).[3] Long-term goals are excellent for establishing direction and vision; in many cases, smaller sub-goals are required so a person can see progress over time.

Hope is a process through which individuals actively pursue their goals, even when things seem to be going their way. By catering to the process of hope even when times are going well, negative effects of stressful events are readily repelled.[4] Furthermore, hope has a tremendous impact on performance above and beyond other positive feelings of self-efficacy, optimism and passion.[5] Self-efficacy, for example, is narrowly focused on one's feelings of capability regarding some situated goal whereas hope is far more pervasive and broad. Hope is "enduring, cross-sectional,

DOI: 10.4324/9781003269038-8

situational, goal-directed."[6] In other words, hope concentrates on more than just the ability to achieve success but on the actual belief that the actions will be initiated and will continue until success is achieved. Where optimism involves the maintenance of an overall belief of success, hope is specifically focused on goal achievement[7,8]

Hope is especially powerful for entrepreneurs. Their entire ventures are built on hope. As a professor of leadership, entrepreneurship and strategy, I've had the opportunity to work with many successful entrepreneurs. For a research project, I was able to be a participant observer with one entrepreneur as he started his lease through the first 15 months of his venture.[9] Many factors helped Bill be successful, but hope is what pulled him through. I gathered his story over 15 months of observing store operations, interviewing key stakeholders, reading social media posts and even talking to customers. I could probably write a book just on his experience. Here is a brief example of how Bill used hope to pull through a very dark and tough time in his first year as an entrepreneur.

Bill, a first-time entrepreneur, was opening a new and used electronic retail store. At 50 years old, he saw this venture as an opportunity to test his capabilities but also as a way to generate financial freedom for himself instead of a corporation. He had been in the industry for many years and was frequently a top performer out of hundreds of other managers. He had been planning for seven years to start his own business but never actually took the step to do so. When he began socializing the idea of opening his own business, the response he got most often was "It's about time!" He knew what he was doing, and he was excited to do it, but there was some added financial stress to opening an entrepreneurial venture.

After 30 years of working, Bill hadn't amassed a lot of wealth. His home was just a few years away from being paid off, but his retirement funds were insufficient for a comfortable post-work life, and his cars needed repairs. He would be putting the little bit he had into this business and getting a home equity loan to start his business. His self-efficacy was high. He knew that he could build a successful business, but his stress was extremely high. At his age and at his point in his career, he doubted he could easily recover. Additionally, he loved this business. He had been in the new and used electronics field for his whole career. He had no desire to do anything else, but if the business failed, he didn't want to go back to working for an electronic retail corporation. If his business failed, he wouldn't just lose the money; he would also lose his dream job. It was an all-or-nothing scenario, but it was a risk he was willing to take. Then he signed the lease.

Bill signed a lease on a great location in thriving town in Arizona. He conducted hours of research interviewing other store employees and customers in the strip mall. He sat and counted cars at the intersection. He felt right about the spot and decided to move forward. The least negotiations were higher than he wanted them to be, but he felt right about the spot. He signed. That's when he stopped sleeping.

Wow . . . so this is it. I guess there's no turning back now. Seven years of planning, and it's finally happening. I sure hope I don't screw this up.

The store finally opened on December 30, 2014.

The first six months were mostly good. Bill was glad to be able to quit is other job and focus all of his attention on his new store. His employees enjoyed having him there. Bill is friendly and fun to be around. The customers enjoyed seeing Bill on a regular basis. Revenue continued to grow. It seemed the store was on the right track to be successful in this extremely competitive environment, but there was a problem. Despite the growing business, the store was still breaking even. The bank account wasn't growing. His friends and family all assured him that this was normal for a first-year business but not for Bill. His life was on the line. This store had to be profitable, or he could lose his house and his reputation. He pushed forward, spending even more time at the store, working open to close nearly every day.

He would arrive home after a 12-hour shift and jump online to research the latest trends. There were several days in a row when Bill would average just three to four hours of sleep. He had a plan in place, though. He was committed to the goal and plan. He continued to push forward with promotions and sales. The revenue continued to grow, but in May, his business was in the red. After all of his work and effort, his business was losing money. The stress continued to mount.

June, July and August were extremely rough. He pushed hard. More sales. More attempts to save money. More marketing and advertising but to no avail. Revenue dipped. Profit dipped more. Bill lost money in June, July and August. He wasn't very fun to be around. He wasn't very fun to talk to. My favorite two reviews that sum up Bill's attitude in August were these:

This place was ok in the beginning, but every time I go in, the manager has a sh***y face. . . .

I stopped in again to see if anything interesting had come in. I left even less impressed than my last visit. Upon entering, I noticed by the video games four stacks of records each around four feet high. Seeing that makes me uncomfortable to buy any records there. Not only that, but the records in the bins are still not organized. How can they expect people to look through every single record? Back when actual record stores still existed, everything was alphabetized, with cards in between with the artists name. . . . The store has potential, but I can't see it lasting too long unless they change their business practice.

Hope, as previously described, has two facets: willpower and waypower, which are encapsulated in The Unity Formula with focus and direction. Bill was watching his store fail, but he didn't know what to do. He still had a goal that he was desperately striving to achieve, but Bill could not see a path forward. Nothing he did seemed to work. It almost seemed as if the store was destined to fail, and who can fight destiny, right? He felt he was losing his store, his home, his dream job and his identity. Part of him wanted to give up. He was just going through the motions, unsure of what to do. Nothing worked. Having the coolest electronics store in town seemed out of reach. He felt hope was lost.

He didn't give up. Late one evening in August, he came to a realization. The holidays were coming! For retail, the holidays are everything. One of the reasons Black Friday is called Black Friday because every retail store in the nation goes in the black, meaning they show profit. If he had a good enough showing during the holidays, then he would be able to attract a host of new customers that would help him to be profitable in the following year. He had experienced more than 30 Black Fridays in his work experience. He knew what he had to do. He created a plan. He could attain the goal. He had a clear path again. Hope restored!

The change in the store from that day to the next was immediate. He was more encouraging with his team members, getting them onboard and excited for the holiday season. He was a joy to be around, joking around with the customers. He was hopeful, but his financial issues weren't resolved yet. He was dangerously close to being out of money, so he maxed out his credit cards, but it didn't bother him because he believed he was on the right path.

Hope is powerful like that. When we feel like we have hope, we move forward despite the consequences, despite the dangers because there's a chance for success. We do it because we want the reward. We have made up our minds to achieve it, and we have a doable plan set forth to make it. Bill's hope drove him to risk even more. His bet had paid off.

Bill was right. The holiday season did put his store the map. Revenues and profits set records. His bank account was replenished, his credit cards were paid off and the customers continued to visit his store after the holiday season. The store is still in operation today. It survived the pandemic and is going strong.

When a group unifies, they become more hopeful. As they grow more committed to the goal and strategy, the strength and fortitude of the team help increase the overall "willpower." Their confidence and commitment to the goal and the plan give increase the overall feeling of "waypower." The team has a goal and while they may not know every step on how to reach the goal, they know the next steps and are committed to moving forward and feel confident that those next steps will lead to next steps.

They are confident in each other as well, that if they reach a point that they cannot overcome alone then their team will be there to give them support. Team willpower and waypower (hope) is extremely powerful for goal accomplishment.

Notes

1. Avey, J. B., Reichard, R. J., Luthans, F., & Mhatre, K. H. (2011). Meta-analysis of the impact of positive psychological capital on employee attitudes, behaviors, and performance. *Human Resource Development Quarterly*, 22(2), 127–152.
2. Gwinn, C., & Hellman, C. M. (2019). *Hope rising: How the science of hope can change your life*. Morgan James Publishing.
3. Gwinn, C., & Hellman, C. M. (2019). *Hope rising: How the science of hope can change your life*. Morgan James Publishing.
4. Valle, M. F., Huebner, E. S., & Suldo, S. M. (2006). An analysis of hope as a psychological strength. *Journal of School Psychology*, 44(5), 393–406.
5. Reichard, R. J., Avey, J. B., Lopez, S., & Dollwet, M. (2013). Having the will and finding the way: A review and meta-analysis of hope at work. *The Journal of Positive Psychology*, 8(4), 292–304.
6. Snyder, C. R. (2002). Hope theory: Rainbows in the mind. *Psychological Inquiry*, 13(4), 249–275.
7. Luthans, F., Youssef, C. M., & Avolio, B. J. (2007). Psychological capital: Investing and developing positive organizational behavior. *Positive Organizational Behavior*, 1(2), 9–24.
8. Peterson, S. J., & Byron, K. (2008). Exploring the role of hope in job performance: Results from four studies. *Journal of Organizational Behavior: The International Journal of Industrial, Occupational and Organizational Psychology and Behavior*, 29(6), 785–803.
9. Ross, J., Strevel, H., & Javadizadeh, B. (2020). Don't stop believin': The journey to entrepreneurial burnout and back again. *Journal of Small Business & Entrepreneurship*, 1–24.

Chapter 5

Unity Component #3—Trust

Trust is my favorite component to discuss because it is the secret sauce to extraordinary teams (ETs). The trust I'm referring to is not the trust where you feel you can leave your valuables with another person and have confidence that they'll still be there when you return. That's a good trust to have, and I would argue that is also important on a team, but this trust is slightly different. I'm referring to *social trust*.

Social trust is when team members not only feel a genuine connection but when they also feel comfortable being around each other. They feel comfortable being themselves around the rest of the team. They aren't afraid to share their agreement or disagreement with ideas. They're okay with being vulnerable with their team and when their team members are vulnerable with them. Social trust is extremely powerful for maximizing team performance.

It's important to note the difference between feeling comfortable in the workplace and feeling socially comfortable. You can feel comfortable without feeling socially comfortable. You can feel socially comfortable without being comfortable. Imagine you've been at a company for ten years. You've worked there a long time. You know everyone there. It's predictable. It pays your bills. You do well there. It's well lit with comfy chairs. They even provide snacks. You're comfortable, but you might not be socially comfortable. You might still keep to yourself. You still don't really participate in meetings. You still don't really have any good friends at work, but it's work, and it's okay. You're comfortable here.

Feeling comfortable is great, but social trust is the most important. When social trust is strong among your team, you'll see great things happen.

Here are some questions to reflect on as you consider the level of trust you have in your team:

- Do you trust a group enough to be your whole self; to share about your family, your hard times and your happy times; to show pictures

DOI: 10.4324/9781003269038-9

of your dog; to tell stories of your partner; or to dress the way you like to dress (within reason of course; it is a place of business)?

- Do you feel comfortable enough to share your ideas, thoughts, suggestions and creativity with the team without fear of being judged?
- If someone does not like your idea, do you trust the team enough to know that it isn't because they don't like you but rather that they don't think it's right for accomplishing the goal at this moment?

The surprising answer for a lot of teams I work with is no. Most do not trust their teams socially, at least not with a good level of security. This deficit brings tremendous team implications, which is really unfortunate because those that are connected and have social trust with their teammates enjoy work far more.

According to a 2022 global culture report,[1] when employees feel high levels of connection and social trust experience tremendous benefits compared with their unconnected counterparts:

- Almost 500% greater workplace experience
- 400% more likely to feel united at work
- 200% more likely to handle stress better
- 170% more likely to produce better work
- And 80% less likely to experience burnout, a real threat to workplace success

With statistics like this, it's easy to see why a group should focus on increasing the social trust in a team.

I call social trust the "secret sauce" to ETs because despite what the countless books and articles say, trust is not required for a team to reach a certain level of success, yet it's crucial to reach the highest levels of unity. As I've shared, you can have a team that accomplishes goals and wins awards without trust. Absolutely, you can. It happens all the time. Think of the teams you've been a part of. You've probably been a part of many teams where you don't even know everyone's name, much less their likes and dislikes, where team members appear sluggish and apathetic toward each other and work—yet you've accomplished your goals and moved on.

The truth is many teams may not require the highest levels of trust in order to get the job done, and that's okay. But if they want the benefits of being an ET, then they'll need the highest levels of trust.

Where else does trust matter—or not? Retail employees do not need high levels of trust to meet sales goals. A manufacturing company does not need the highest levels of trust to meet day-to-day standards. Hospitals, athletic organizations, entertainment industries, retail stores, classrooms, families, church groups, charitable organizations, marriages and friends do not *need* high levels of trust to get the job done. By this I mean they can accomplish some tasks without trust. But to truly thrive, innovate and create an ET with a positive and enjoyable team culture, trust becomes crucial.

Many companies compensate for low levels of trust by throwing more people and resources at a project. A small team with higher levels of social trust can outperform a large team without social trust just about any day of the week. *Teams will never reach their full potential without social trust.* Such a bold statement deserves some clarification.

Common Misperceptions About Trust

Before we dive too much deeper into trust, there are some common misconceptions about trust that we need to resolve before moving forward.

First, at some time in your life, you have probably heard a phrase similar to "Trust takes years to build and seconds to lose." This is false. Majorly false. Like, how-did-this-even-become-a-thing false. To challenge this phrase, consider these situations:

- Have you ever met someone you connected with immediately? Someone who within hours, you felt like you wanted to hang out with that person, invite them over to your house, go mini-golfing with them or do some other activity together?
- Have you ever shared something intimate with someone that you've barely known for more than a day? Your dreams, ideas, creativity, five-year plan? Things you normally wouldn't share with people?

Most people have. This is directly in contrast to the common saying, "It takes years to build trust."

In fact, you've likely built trust with someone in *hours*. That's because trust is not a fancy saying. It's science.

Physical Versus Social Trust

Trust is compartmentalized into several subtopics. The two clearest compartments are *physical* and *social*.

Physical is the trust we have that people will take care of the physical parts of our lives. Two common examples might be safety and money. We might trust that someone is not going to physically hurt us or steal our valuables. This is the most basic level of trust and is commonly felt with most of the people we encounter in the workplace or groups that we willingly join.

Social trust means we feel comfortable being ourselves—even if that means revealing some of our weaknesses. It involves trusting others not just with shared activities but also with shared dreams, ideas and goals. It means sharing our quirks without fear of judgement. We can be ourselves. We can receive and give feedback openly because team members trust that team members have the best intentions and that no harm is intended.

Some have stated that trust is on a scale, with physical trust on the low end of the scale with social trust increasing as one moves up on the scale. Actually, physical and social trust are in separate compartments—related but acting mostly independent of each other.

We can have high physical trust, such as when we enter a theme park. We generally let our guard down because we trust the people around us not to hurt us or steal from us. We all went through a metal detector. We're all smiling and having a good time. Parents leave their strollers parked where anyone could walk off with them. We are most likely feeling high levels of physical trust with one another as adults, though we my keep a cautious eye on our children.

However, we wouldn't necessarily feel high levels of social trust at a theme park. We probably wouldn't walk up to a stranger and tell them some of our greatest ideas or pay them compliments or suggest improvements. Imagine what that would be like:

- "Hey there. Hi. Hey there. Quick note on your outfit. The Mickey ears really don't go with your Transformers shirt."
- "Excuse me, your child is crying because she is tired, hungry and has heat exhaustion. She doesn't want more goldfish. She needs to rest. Please don't force her to wait in line with us for the next hour."
- "Excuse me, sir. I know you're trying hard, but could you hurry up? I need to be on the other side of the park in one hour, and I've already been waiting in line for this meal for 25 minutes."

All three of these statements could be said in situations when you have high levels of social trust with very little, if any, repercussion. In fact, some groups with high levels of social trust may laugh at such comments. Think of your best friends. You've probably said worse to them before. When we feel comfortable with people, we can be honest and open because they know we're not being intentionally difficult. They trust that we are not trying to hurt them, and we trust that they will not judge us for what we're saying.

Given that we are all in a theme park and thus we all have similar interests (family, fun, escapism, high ticket prices, long lines, churros, Dole Whips, rides and crowds), we are likely to form shallow social bonds quickly, but we probably do not have the deepest levels of social trust with everyone.

Physical trust is a required element with our teammates, but social trust is what creates team unity. It's the invisible glue that binds people despite challenges or setbacks.

Project Aristotle: A Study in Psychological Safety and Performance[2]

Not only have I discovered the importance of social trust time and time again in creating team unity and leading to ETs, but Google spent millions of dollars and years to make the same discovery. (They should've just called me! I would've told them.)

Google is a data company. They not only track the data of countless consumers, but they also had been collecting performance data on its own employees. Google even has a department dedicated to analyzing how to maximize output from its employees. Perhaps this sounds like a dystopian, Big Brother society, but the results of this data collection allowed Google to apply incredible innovations for workplace benefits and trainings for workplace behavior. Programs like this have secured Google as one of the top places to work year after year.

Despite their forward thinking in workplace offerings, the concept of "the perfect team," a team with maximum levels of effectiveness and efficiency, inspired them to devote more resources to the project. Google was expanding its digital empire and had teams around the world. Some of their teams weren't performing as great as Google knew they could. Many were great, reliable teams that got the job done, but some excelled far beyond expectations.

In 2012, the company started Project Aristotle to study the intricacies of teams. They decided to invest in discovering what made great teams great. The name Aristotle was chosen because of his famous quote "The whole is greater than the sum of its parts."

Setting Up the Study

The best researchers, statisticians and psychologists were gathered for the program. The first assignment was simple. "What makes an effective team?" Being a group of analyzers, they analyzed each word in their first task. Two words stood out, "effective" and "team."

Google quickly realized that there should be a difference between *work groups* and *teams*.

- Work groups have very little interdependence. They're people working together but not actively and consistently relying on each other for progress and direction.

- Teams are interdependent. Team members need each other to progress.

Once that was defined, their next task was to define the term *effective*. Different levels in the organization defined effective in different ways.

- *Executives* defined effective by the numbers a team achieved. Being a programming company, they looked at lines of code written, bugs created, punctuality, customer satisfaction, financial contribution, etc. In other words, the executive largely focused on task performance.
- *Team members* weighted output less than culture. They agreed that output mattered, but the contribution to the team as a whole mattered to them most. They focused more on conceptual performance as the biggest contributor to team effectiveness.
- The *team leader* was in the middle. They saw merit in looking at task performance but also saw the importance of team culture and conceptual performance.

Team Aristotle decided that their measurements had to be both qualitative and quantitative. They ended up measuring team effectiveness in four ways:

1. Executive evaluation of the team
2. Team leader evaluation of the team
3. Team member evaluation of the team
4. Sales performance against quarterly quota

Once the performance measure was set up, they identified 180 teams around the world to be their subjects. They collected team effectiveness data as outlined, along with over 250 additional items. In other words, Team Aristotle decided to conduct one of the most extensive team studies ever conducted in recent history. They engaged their statisticians that ran over 35 statistical models and paired the results with qualitative data. The data were inconclusive.

What's in Google's Secret Sauce?

This is similar to what I mentioned earlier regarding social trust. That is, I also had a difficult time nailing down the specific "secret ingredient" in teamwork because social trust can look different on each team.

Despite looking at the massive amounts of data in a variety of ways, Google discovered no patterns or similarities between extraordinary teams. What did stand out is that there didn't seem to be a particular personality trait, knowledge, skill or workplace behavior that made an impact. Some teams had friends that socialized outside of work. Other teams did not socialize outside of work. Some teams appeared to be very organized with a strong leader. Others were less organized and had some-one who resembled a facilitator, or they shared leadership among them-selves. Then, other data points showed two teams with extremely similar makeups but very different levels of effectiveness. A natural pattern did not seem to exist.

Google continued researching. They were intrigued by research on *norms* or commonly understood behaviors on a team. Norms are not written rules but rather traditions and standards that the team tends to follow. A person can act one way as a person but act very differently on a team because the norms are to behave in a different way than one might as an individual. Intrigued, team Aristotle reviewed the data again, spe-cifically looking at the team's norms.

They uncovered more data points to consider. Some teams commu-nicated frequently. Others did not. Some had loud, open debates about products and direction, while others remained more reserved. Some teams required order and politeness in conversations; others allowed interruptions. Some celebrated birthdays. Some discussed outside events. Again, there was no clear connection between team norms and team suc-cess. Ineffective and effective teams had shared behaviors that seemed to contribute to both success and failure. For example, they found both ineffective and effective teams communicated, and both followed set tra-ditions or norms.

The researchers seemed to be missing the key differentiating factor between effective and ineffective teams. While no clear path was clearly evident, they did feel like they were closer to discovering the secret sauce to team effectiveness.

The team reviewed the qualitative data again with the new lens, focus-ing on behaviors, but instead found several comments about how people felt.

How Do Feelings Factor Into Team Performance? Hint: They Are a Big Deal

Feelings frequently accompany our interactions with people. Sometimes we like someone because we feel good around them. Sometimes we don't like someone because something may seem off. Whether or not we act on our feelings, we are quite in tune with our feelings about people and groups. Our emotional memories allow us to recall many team experi-ences so well.

Emotional memories are when the mind "tags" an event as different or unique because the emotion was stronger.[3] Think of your biggest, most impactful memories in life. Not only are they easy to remember, but the emotions experienced during the creation of those memories can probably be recalled quite easily as well. This might seem quite obvious for big impactful memories, but think about smaller, seemingly insignificant memories from your childhood when you experienced heightened emotions. What comes to mind? Are they easy to recall?

Being on a great, unified team elicits many great, emotionally "tagged" memories. Google began noticing that feelings played an important role in the most successful, unified teams.

Members on the highest performing teams felt safe to share their feelings and emotions—and did so frequently. Team members who trusted their leaders and team members not to judge their actions felt like they could take risks. These teams were the most effective.

On the contrary, team members who felt judged at every decision stayed quiet and only fulfilled the minimum for fear of getting into trouble. These teams did not perform as highly.

This, along with other findings, signaled to Team Aristotle that *psychological safety (part of social trust)* was the most important factor in creating an effective team. Secret sauce confirmed!

Team Aristotle reported their findings and saw immediate results. It was difficult at first because the manner in which social trust is created on a team is different for every team. But as leaders and team members opened up about their lives, they realized that others began to feel comfortable doing the same. The result was teams being interested in each other and sharing ideas. This created critical outcomes for an innovative company.

Psychological safety is only a part of social trust, however. Simply being vulnerable, as project Aristotle suggests, doesn't necessarily lead to better teams. It's being vulnerable and allowing other people to be vulnerable as Google discovered, but it's more. It's taking social risks by sharing ideas, providing feedback and allowing ourselves to be quirky. It's a team that is free of social judgement. Psychological safety is a great and important start!

Social Trust Engages People—and Increases Performance

We've discussed the importance of social trust in order to create a positive environment for ideas, but it is also critical that a team have social trust to help everyone feel connected because when we feel connected, we are more willing to invest our whole selves into a project. When a team feels connected, they are far more willing to give it their all.

Rowing is an extremely popular sport around the world—and one that relies on social trust. While its popularity has declined over decades, it's still one of the most watched Olympic events. The sport is probably one of the least understood as well.

Rowing seems quite simple. You row. Do that over and over and you go somewhere fast. Do that fast enough and you win. Simple, right? Well, this team sport is a bit more complex than that.

In the 1930s, rowing was one of the top sports in the world. Tens of thousands would show up to a rowing event. It was seen as the ultimate sport requiring the ultimate athletes to compete.

Rowing requires that just about every muscle in the body be at peak performance for a grueling six minutes. The amount of strain that a rower endures in a two-kilometer, six-minute-ish race is more than what many basketball players endure in an entire game. So much strain endured in such a short amount of time puts a tremendous strain on the body, which leads to many potential injuries, but the rowers can't stop. Each rower must continue rowing because seven other rowers are depending on the teammate to continue his or her performance. The slightest decline in performance from a single player can put the entire boat in a sharp decline. Rowers have to trust each other, and to do this, they need to feel connected.

A Lack of Social Trust Hurts Team Performance

Joe Rantz was a poor, rugged young man from Sequim, Washington (later of *Twilight* fame), when he tried out for the rowing team in 1934.[4] His mother died when he was only three years old. His father remarried two years later to a young woman. In a very short amount of time, she decided she did not care much for Joe. Within a year, she began having children of her own and decided that Joe got in the way of raising her own children. At the age of 10, Joe was sent away to live with the school-master. He felt out of place and spent most of his time exploring the vast wilderness. At the age of 15, his father, stepmother and four step-siblings moved away, leaving Joe on his own. He cut wood, removed stumps and bailed hay for money; fished and planted gardens for food; and still maintained good grades in all of his lessons at school. He was a loner and found it difficult to trust those around him. He kept to himself in school.

His senior year, he was invited to live with his uncle's family, where he attended a more prestigious high school. There, he excelled in everything he did and became an accomplished gymnast. The University of Washington (UW) crew coach saw him perform. He invited him to try out for the UW crew team. Joe accepted and moved that summer.

Joe progressed quickly through the ranks of his UW crew team. Rowing is a spring sport, which meant the fall was a long and strenuous tryout. Close to 200 young men tried out for the few spots on the row team. Joe took pride in knowing that his rough life prepared him to excel. The practices were daily, intense and often cold rain-or-shine events. This convinced many young men who came from a more comfortable life to quit.

Joe was ecstatic to learn he made the team, but he looked at the accomplishment as evidence of his strength and endurance. At the time, he cared little about his teammates.

Joe didn't have the financial resources that a stable family could provide a young college freshman. On top of his grueling rowing practices, Joe also worked as a janitor and musician, playing in a performing group in the evenings. Even with his summer work and two jobs, he was still barely making enough to get by. He wore the same clothes nearly every day. They were becoming ragged. The crew members made fun of him, reinforcing the chasm that Joe already felt existed between him and the rest of the crew. He felt disconnected. He came from a very unique background. He knew it and appreciated it. The rest of the team made Joe a target because of it. He never quite felt comfortable in his crew. He worked hard and did as he was asked, but he had difficulty trusting his teammates in social situations. His manners were rough. Theirs were more refined.

Joe was part of the team, but he perceived the differences to be so great that he felt he didn't fit in. Joe didn't feel comfortable enough to socially trust his team members. As far as work ethic goes, Joe was an excellent member of the team. His strength and determination to win matched or exceeded those of any of his teammates.

But he was sloppy. He didn't know the proper techniques.

The coaches worked with Joe to refine his rowing ability with great success. They won several key matches, but the team's performance was not dependable. In one match, they'd set the course record; then in another match, they'd barely pull anything together.

Joe was put on several teams at several different shell levels (varsity, junior varsity etc.). He continued to impress the coaches, but Joe still struggled to gel with a team.

Coach Bolles frequently reminded the teams about the need to function as a team, pushing them to hit their *swing*—the picture of team unity. Swing is when a row team is at perfect harmony. It's more difficult than it sounds. The team changes row rates throughout the race. A team in full swing can react to the changes together, applying the same amount of pressure so they move as one. Their oars are in complete alignment. They're 100% following the coxswain's orders. They're dipping the oars in the water at the same depth. They're moving together. They're breathing in unison. When a team reaches full swing, they become *extraordinary*, and their performance dramatically increases.

Swing is the ideal situation, but to reach it, team members must work together, matching each other's ability like a choir singing in unison. There is no room for independence.

Joe's team was still eight independent oarsmen who worked together, but they weren't unified. To achieve success, they'd have to learn to think and work as one.

The coach challenged the team members to get to know each other.

The summer between Joe's sophomore and junior year, Joe realized that he and a few of his teammates were employed on a dam project together. Upon getting to know them, he learned that several of his teammates hadn't come from wealthy families as he had previously thought, that they had to work to survive as well. This knowledge helped Joe lower his defenses around them. He found common ground between them and began bonding with them even outside of the boat. With their new friendship, others began accepting Joe for who he was. He began to do the same for them.

But Joe was still missing something. Something was still hurting his performance. His coaches could see it.

His coach, George Pocock, famous for manufacturing racing shells—and for his studious, scientific view of rowing—pulled Joe aside and gave him this advice: "Joe, when you really start trusting those other boys, you will feel a power at work within you that is far beyond anything you've ever imagined. Sometimes, you will feel as if you have rowed right off the planet and are rowing among the stars."

Joe realized that he had given himself over to rowing but not over to his teammates. Rowing, Joe realized, was a symphony. He was just a member in the symphony, and together they had to play the song that none of them independently could play at the same level. Joe, someone who had spent so many years depending on his own efforts and his own ability, realized that he had to open himself up, even if it meant getting hurt. He wanted his teammates to accept him as he was, but he wasn't accepting them for who they were. He assumed because they appeared to be different from him that they would judge him. Ironically, he was the one judging them.

He wanted trust but realized he had to reciprocate it.

In early 1936, the row teams knew their coach hoped to have a UW team in the Olympics. Of the several row teams or "shells" competing at UW, only the first shell would represent UW at the Olympic tryouts. Joe was consistently racing in third shell. He continued to work with Pocock, who noticed great potential with Joe. Joe made improvements, and by March, Joe moved to the first shell.

Joe knew most of his teammates, but this time he opened himself up to them—getting to know them and spending the little extra time he had with them. With this new level of social trust, they became a team, and for the first time, Joe recognized the feeling of unity he felt with his team was what George had been talking about.

The results were obvious. In their first race together, they won by a staggering seven boat lengths. Coach Pocock selected Joe's shell to represent UW in the Olympic tryouts.

At the Olympic tryouts, the varsity team from UW continued to win. Some teams go a whole regatta without hitting their swing, but the boys from UW hit their swing in every race and handily won a spot on the Olympic team. It was a tremendous victory for everyone involved but especially the eight team members who all came from modest upbringings. They were going to Germany to represent the United States in Berlin!

Becoming and remaining an ET requires constant effort. Just because your team has reaching extraordinary levels doesn't mean it will remain there indefinitely. It requires effort to maintain such high levels of focus, direction and trust.

Upon arriving in Berlin, the team struggled again. They couldn't seem to catch their stride. They were losing focus, direction—and trust. They began doubting that they were capable of competing on the world stage. They doubted themselves. They doubted their teammates. They didn't discuss their fears, however. They bottled them up and hid them away, instead choosing to focus on the numerous distractions surrounding them.

They also began to lose focus and direction, visiting Berlin almost daily and enjoying the food and drink. They exercised less and even gained weight. As they explored, they met athletes from over 30 countries around the world. This was an incredible opportunity for the team from UW. Many of them had never been out of the Northwest. Now they were in a cornucopia of distractions, perfect for eight terrified young men.

Just a few days before their event, they found themselves alone and undistracted by the life outside their hotel room. Finally, they faced their fears, admitting one by one that they struggled with dark feelings of unworthiness. They admitted that they were scared. They didn't feel like they belonged in the Olympics. They were just a bunch of regular guys from UW. *What business did they have competing in the Olympics?* They were suffering from a real psychological instance called *imposter syndrome.*

Imposter Syndrome Can Derail Social Trust

Imposter syndrome is when we feel we're going to get caught any moment for the fraud that we believe we are.[5] It's a common feeling, but imposter syndrome discredits all the effort and energy that we put into achieving our status. It is a unity detractor and a social trust destroyer. It can make us feel emotions similar to depression, unworthy of success or belonging. Many have described imposter syndrome as feelings of "just getting lucky" with success—and that eventually the "imposter" would be uncovered for the fraud that they are. These feelings can cause a person to clam up and become unwilling to share with those around them.

Imposter syndrome hit these young rowers hard. They felt they were out of their league. They felt every other team, especially the German and English teams, were awesome—but that the UW team was made up of just normal people. As they opened up, they became vulnerable.

Vulnerability helped them to realize that they couldn't do it alone. They needed each other. As they shared their feelings, they also shared their burden of carrying these feelings. They didn't have to carry them alone anymore. The decided that they would face these feelings together. The team rebuilt social trust and decided if they were going to compete, then they would give it their all physically, mentally and emotionally.

The result was dramatic. Germany dominated the Olympics that year. They won 89 medals in 1936, 30-plus more than their closest competitor, the United States. In rowing, Germany and England were the heavy favorites. Both countries had a long history dominating the sport. Seven rowing events were held. Germany won five gold medals, England won one but the United States won the gold medal for the eight-man rowing team by team from UW. The book *Boys in the Boat* chronicles the story in great detail.

Trust is the secret sauce to creating unity in ETs. Without trust, team members will withhold ideas, and they'll also withhold effort and resist full interdependence. Teams can perform without trust, but they won't reach full potential without it.

Notes

1. Tanner Institute, O. C. (2021). (rep.). 2022 global culture report. OC Tanner Institute. Retrieved from www.octanner.com/content/dam/oc-tanner/images/v2/culture-report/2022/home/INT-GCR2022.pdf
2. Duhigg, C. (2016, February 25). What Google learned from its quest to build the perfect team. *The New York Times*. www.nytimes.com/2016/02/28/magazine/what-google-learned-from-its-quest-to-build-the-perfect-team.html?_r=0
3. Richter-Levin, G., & Akirav, I. (2003). Emotional tagging of memory formation in the search for neural mechanisms. *Brain Research Reviews, 43*(3), 247–256.
4. Brown, D. J. (2021). *The boys in the boat: Nine Americans and their epic quest for gold at the 1936 Berlin Olympics*. Penguin Books.
5. Bothello, J., & Roulet, T. J. (2018). The imposter syndrome, or the misrepresentation of self in academic life. *Journal of Management Studies, 56*(4), 854–861.

Research Note: Focus and Trust = Creativity, Innovation and Inspiration

When a team is intently focused on a goal and has high levels of social trust, it leads to amazing results. Such a team is passionate for goal attainment and committed to overcoming any barrier. This causes team members to think "outside the box" at home and at work for any solution that may work. Creativity rarely happens when a team is not committed to a goal and when high levels of social trust are not present.[1]

Disney and Universal benefit from focus and social trust with their theme park designs. The Disney Imagineers and the Universal Creative Team are frequently given complex projects that require unique and innovative ideas. Their ideas eventually turn into thrilling rides and attractions that are enjoyed by families from around the world.

But the ideas don't just happen. They start with a group of people committed to creating a great attraction being given an abstract task requiring high levels of social trust to complete.

An amusement park's focus is on entertaining through thrills. It's all about the rides and the fun. Think of Six Flags, King's Island or Cedar Point. Ride designs are complex at amusement parks, but a traveling rollercoaster salesperson can swing by and show you the newest coaster. If you like it, you could paint it black and call it a Batman ride. I'm oversimplifying, but this example is not too far off the mark. If you took out the rides of an amusement park, you wouldn't have much left.

Theme parks, on the other hand, depend on the story. They rely on the ohhhs and ahhhs as guests explore the intricate detail painstakingly developed for their entertainment. They want their guests to feel as if they're part of the story. They don't just add a ride to a theme park; they have to theme a ride at a theme park. It has to be designed with a story and then encapsulated in an amusing scene, which is normally nestled in a land. It adds another level of complexity to the design, but that's the point.

If you take the rides out of an amusement park, not much is left. If you take the rides out of a theme park, you still have a theme park that would be very enjoyable to walk around. Disney's Epcot is a great example.

DOI: 10.4324/9781003269038-10

They're expanding the ride offerings, but Epcot was originally built without many rides. It was designed as more of a living museum.

To design a ride at a theme park, it starts with a brainstorming session. Disney refers to it as *blue sky*—meaning the sky is the limit on how what is on the table. Some refer to it as *ideation*—the collection of a lot of ideas with the understanding that the feasibility of these ideas will be evaluated at a later date. Whether you're Merlin Studios, Disney World or Universal Creative, the rules are the same. No idea is a bad idea. If you self-censor for fear that your idea is bad or it might be made fun of, then you're hurting the team.[2]

It's probably not too difficult to imagine what a brainstorming session would be like without social trust. You've probably either seen it or, unfortunately, experienced it.

BOSS: Okay, looking for good ideas for a new widget. Any ideas? We're going to put them up on this board. Yes, what was your name again? Okay, yes, you.

PERSON A: I was thinking we could create a widget that makes breakfast.

BOSS: Okay . . . maybe . . . Okay, someone else.

PERSON B: Maybe there could be a widget that makes lunch?

BOSS (EXASPERATED): Okay, people, listen. I need some real ideas here. C'mon, give me your best.

PERSON C (TIMIDLY): Maybe a widget that makes dinner?

BOSS (RUBBING HIS EYES): Okay, well, those were great ideas. Listen over there at Make-a-lot, they're making this new widget that does XYZ. What if we had a widget that did WXYZ? Wouldn't that be great?

Situations like this fabricated one are far too frequent in the workplace. The leader comes in and really is looking for confirmation that their idea is the best. Every other idea gets shot down. Everyone is in the room guessing what the boss is thinking. The first person to guess it wins the boss's favor.

Situations like these can take many different forms, but they all end up the same. Focus and trust decrease. Creativity is diminished. Engagement is squashed.

What many leaders and facilitators may not understand is that all ideas are important, even the bad ones. One bad idea might spark an idea that leads to a great idea. Ever looked at the user instructions for a microwave? It's filled with cautions and warnings. You'd think we were using nuclear energy to heat and reheat our food. Many people thought microwaves in homes were a terrible idea at first, but someone had a crazy idea.[3] That idea was modified into a usable idea. The group needs to trust each other in order to share ideas, even the seemingly bad ones.

The need for social trust cannot be overstated when designing the next ride or attraction. The discussions last for weeks or even months. According to Designer Joe Rohde, executive designer and vice president at Walt Disney Imagineering, when Disney's team was designing the Animal Kingdom park in Orlando, Florida, they spent weeks just talking about the concept of the park.

> We spent two weeks doing nothing but talking through the implication of the word *animal*. What does it mean? What emotions does it convey, and what activities does it imply? We had to determine how broad the word would be defined to tell us what would be included and excluded from the project. We also had to consider what happens when you put *Disney* alongside the word. We then put the word *kingdom* at the end and had to determine how to turn those three words into a place—and what kind of place it would be. We literally scribbled on hundreds of index cards before we boiled it all down to a philosophical proposal—if we are going to do a park about animals, and it is a Disney park, then it needed to be more than just live animals.[4]

The initial brainstorming stages can take many weeks, but that's only the beginning.

After the initial idea phase, then it goes to conceptual design—when the writing, illustrations, research and model-making occur. A classic example of this is in the story boards, when animators pitch the ideas to a room of people vying for approval to continue with their direction.

From there, the idea moves to feasibility, when operations meets the creative team. Here, they have to figure out how the idea is going to work, how many people are going to be able to pass through the attraction an hour, what the maintenance costs and initial build costs are going to be.

Next, if everything has worked out, it moves to design development, when the idea comes to life. They get the money to move forward a step at a time.

The attraction then moves to installation and is finally handed to the operations team.

During any of these steps, it is critical that people speak up if they see something to address because a successful project benefits the company, the hundreds of employees working on the project and the thousands or millions who will end up enjoying the project throughout its lifespan. Focus is necessary to keep the creative team on track for a spectacular design. Social trust is a must in order to provide the ideas and engagement necessary for a creative endeavor.

When a team has high levels of focus and trust, they are willing to share ideas feelings and thoughts regardless of how silly they may sound. These thoughts and ideas build off each other. Many times the creations cause fits of laughter at the absurdity of some of the ideas like a group of friends trying to think of names for their new band. But, occasionally, these ideas gel and morph into a beautiful and useful picture of a new creation. This is called *collective creativity*. It requires focus and trust.

Creativity Is Needed in All Organizations, Not Just the Obviously "Creative" Ones

Several examples of collective creativity have been used. As described, theme park designs depend on it. New movies require it. We often think of creativity as applied to artistic endeavors, but creativity applies to business as well. Norton Healthcare System in Louisville, Kentucky faced a potentially crippling situation with vaccine distributions, but thanks to a creative software team, they were able to overcome and excel.[5]

> [The COVID-19 vaccine distribution] completely changed the paradigm of how people had approached healthcare. Never before have we had a demand issue. Remember, most people defer their healthcare decisions until things become a real issue. For the first time in history, we had people seeking health care services with a higher demand than a new shiny Apple product.
>
> (Gabe Riggs, Norton Healthcare, Director of Enterprise Applications and Software Development)

The process of distributing vaccines was complex. Each patient would need two appointments, one for each shot. Hundreds of locations would need to be appropriately staffed with the appropriate amount of vaccines. Because of the extremely strict storage requirements for the vaccines, if too many vaccines were unthawed for distribution than needed, then they would be wasted. If there were too few, then there would be angry customers. There also needed to be a verification process to ensure people weren't trying to "cheat" the system.

The situation continued to intensify. January numbers continued to increase by 10% each week for the next four weeks. As more and more people trusted the vaccine, the vaccine request increased. Over 100,000 people were receiving injections every week. Many hospitals were using their websites to facilitate vaccine appointments, but the sharp increase in numbers stressed the system. Hospital sites in Michigan, Indiana, Massachusetts, Florida, Pennsylvania, Texas, Alabama, Mississippi, Kentucky and most other states experienced crashes due to cyber-attacks, duplicate appointments, scams and overwhelming interest in the vaccine. An immediate solution was needed.

Previously used methods weren't working. A new, creative solution was needed to handle the increasing volume. Norton Healthcare looked to Gabe for answers. Gabe looked to his team. High levels of focus and trust were required.

"At first, we weren't exactly sure what to do, but we knew what our goal was, and we knew we couldn't fail. We were all on board."

"The hierarchy was out. We were all equals. No ideas were bad ideas. We analyzed what we currently had and looked for potential flaws."

Fortunately, this was a team that had been together for several years. They had high levels of trust already. Their team had experienced several successes in the recent past. When they heard of the situation, they willingly stepped up to the challenge together. There were many bad ideas that were quickly sifted through, some ideas that were pursued and later discovered it wouldn't work. There was no judgement. Everyone was pushing forward together. Eventually, after many hours and a few sleepless nights, a new, innovative, creative solution was created. After testing, Norton's site was up and serving thousands without crashes.

"The best part is, after realizing the success of our system, we made it available for free to healthcare facilities everywhere. At least a portion of our software is benefiting Americans across the country."

Since the creation of the system, it has been able to handle hundreds of thousands of appointments. At the time of writing this chapter, 2.7 million Kentucky residents have received at least one shot of the Pfizer, Moderna or Johnson and Johnson vaccine. Many of those appointments were handled nearly flawlessly through the system created by the Norton Healthcare software team.

Creativity in the workplace is obviously required for companies that market their creativity such as theme parks, interior design, bakeries or event production companies, but creativity should be a welcome addition to any team. Creativity comes naturally as teams increase their unity, especially when focus and trust are at their highest points.

Notes

1. Harvey, S. (2014). Creative synthesis: Exploring the process of extraordinary group creativity. *Academy of Management Review*, 39(3), 324–343.
2. Younger, D., & Baxter, T. (2016). *Theme park design: The art of themed entertainment*. Inklingwood Press.
3. Blitz, M. (2021, September 6). There's an incredible story behind how the microwave was invented . . . by accident. *Popular Mechanics*. www.popularmechanics.com/technology/gadgets/a19567/how-the-microwave-was-invented-by-accident/
4. Younger, D., & Baxter, T. (2016). *Theme park design: The art of themed entertainment*. Inklingwood Press.
5. Ross, J. (2021, June 14). Norton healthcare's response to COVID vaccine demand. personal.

Chapter 6

Unity Component #4—Conflict

I've stated that *conflict* is one of the four components of unity. Actually, conflict plays a different role in unity than its counterparts focus, direction or trust. Instead, conflict is the great destroyer of unity. It is a negative trait that serves to divide a team's unity. It can detract from focus, direction and trust. It is noticeably absent from extraordinary teams (ETs) and obviously present in dysfunctional teams.

As previously mentioned, I include conflict as a core component just as anyone would include warnings as part of directions in a road trip. Google Maps includes construction updates. My parents are always up to date on the weather. My friends have included warnings about dangerous intersections or the "rough times of night" to be in a location. The warnings are not needed to get from point A to point B, but they're certainly appreciated components in provided instructions and can be lifesavers. Thus, conflict is a necessary discussion point in unity as it is definitely a major warning for anyone looking to increase their team unity to realize ET success.

In The Unity Formula, conflict serves as the denominator. As a denominator, this means the bigger the conflict score, the less unity exists in your team. Managing conflict plays such a critical role in unity that I include it as a core component in unity it as a caution similar to how someone may warn you of dangerous weather when giving directions. *Manage your conflict quick and well because conflict is the great vacuum of success.*

Conflict is no joke. In a 2020 study on workplace conflict,[1] only 22% said workplace conflict really didn't bother them. The other 78% said that workplace conflict caused a dramatic increase in stress (48%), a significant drop in motivation or commitment (40%), a decrease in feelings of self-worth (25%) and quite a drop in productivity (20%). Interestingly, of the thousands surveyed, 80% said their immediate supervisor is the main person that should handle team-related conflict, but only 40% of supervisors reported actually receiving any form of conflict training. This is something to consider when 95% of those who receive any form of conflict resolution training say that it is useful.

DOI: 10.4324/9781003269038-11

The effects of conflict in a team are tremendous: 76% of team members say they avoid other team members they have conflict with; 25% actually admitted to missing days of work because of conflicts among team members.[2] A team that avoids each other is certainly experiencing extreme forms of disunity. Conflict truly causes a severe strain on unity. So, if it's so severe, you may ask, "Okay, so how do I prevent this destroyer in my workplace teams?" Well, according to the reports, the top three ways to handle conflict in order are:

1. Be proactive.
2. Be involved.
3. Be clear.

Good news! We'll discuss these in more detail later but using the unity principles discussed in this book is an excellent step to engaging in all three conflict management techniques!

At a very basic level, a conflict is *a disagreement*. However, there is a bit more to discuss in order to understand conflict that will help in understanding conflict's role in developing extraordinary teams.

Task Conflict Versus Relational Conflict

There are two types of conflict, *task conflict* and *relational conflict*.

- Task conflict is when two people disagree over how to accomplish a task.[3]

Disagreements involving how to accomplish a task often lead to a better result. A simple example is if you and I decided to build a birdhouse together. Why a birdhouse? Well, for some reason, growing up in Fort Worth, Texas, every beginner's project in Cub Scouts seemed to be a birdhouse. I'm not sure if Texas had a shortage of homes for birds that I was unaware of to warrant small children building hundreds of birdhouses. I cannot recall birds sleeping on the ground for lack of housing, but I was young and wasn't up to date on the news, so I guess it is possible that the homeless bird population was more drastic than I realized. Regardless of the bird home shortage issue, a birdhouse is a simple project that requires very little engineering knowledge, which is perfect for a guy like me.

If you and I wanted to build a birdhouse (our *focus* on a goal), we'd most likely disagree initially with the design of the birdhouse (our *direction*). We may even disagree with the materials. But we would talk about our disagreements (demonstrating *trust*), and eventually, we would build a great birdhouse together. Our final product would most likely be a combination of our two ideas. It would be great.

When most people think about conflict in the workplace, they're referring to task conflict, a disagreement over how to approach work. This is often a good conflict to have because it can lead to a greater product overall.

Relational conflict, on the other hand, is not.

- **Relational conflict is interpersonal and often occurs when two people just don't like each other.**[4]

This can be as superficial as a person graduated from a rival university (immature, but I've seen it) to something as deep as feeling professional threats, personality clashes or deep-rooted psychological difference.

Relational Conflict is the Vacuum of Success

Relational conflict is the vacuum of success. It can be overcome, but it is normally not just laughed off. When relational conflict is present, productivity and performance get vacuumed into the void where it wastes away.

Not too long ago, I was at one of my favorite fast-food places. I had been looking forward to going to this place all day. I was busy at lunch, so I waited until 2:00 p.m. to swing by. The entrance was clean and welcoming. The smell was pleasant. There was a person at the register who welcomed me with a smile, ready to take my order.

Sometimes I can be indecisive, so I ask for recommendations. The employee gave a few great recommendations. I put in my order. She even suggested some additional items. I'm a sucker for suggestive sales and upsells. I gladly accepted.

Up to this point, this was an exceptional visit. Then it got exciting.

A few minutes later, two more people came in and ordered: a pregnant woman with a baby in a car seat and a construction worker. A few cars were waiting in the drive-through. The little fast-food restaurant was experiencing a mini-rush.

Given the outstanding performance so far, I felt sure the employees were well-trained in handling rushes. This was slightly different though because it was during shift change, and it was during an unexpected time. Two p.m. is not normally when people rush in for lunch on a Friday.

The attendant up front tried her best to manage the stress, but it was obvious the tension was mounting. She began pacing back and forth, calling out orders. She went to the drive-through employee to ask for help, but he was busy with his line of customers. He recommended she go in back and ask one of the four employees making food for help.

FRONT REGISTER EMPLOYEE (FRE): Can you please come help me up front before you leave? We're getting slammed.

BACK EMPLOYEE: I've already been here eight hours. I'm tired, and my feet hurt. I want to go home.

The powder keg had been lit. *Run! It's going to blow!*

Yelling, flying napkins and things crashing followed. This was one of those fast-food restaurants where the customer cannot see into the back kitchen except through about a 12-inch gap used for the back employees to slide food to the front employees. It was through this gap that the other two customers and I watched the scene unfold between the front register employee, the back employee, three bystanders and a team leader desperately trying to manage the drive-through and the conflict in the back.

FRE: (yelling, throwing things, decibel level: police siren or airplane engine) You NEVER want to help. You ONLY think about yourself! Why do you even work here?!

BE: (muttering calmly and slowly walking, dragging her feet, gathering her things, decibel level: between a normal conversation and a hair dryer) I don't understand why you're yelling. I've worked all day, and I want to go home. I'm tired.

FRE: (still yelling, hitting tables now, pointing fingers) You never want to help out! I ask you for just a little help, and you can't even help for five minutes!

FRE and BE are moving around the back—with the three bystanders shuffling out of the way to avoid the ire of FRE.

BE: (still muttering calmly, not listening, still gathering things and shuffling about) I worked a whole shift. I'm tired, and I just want to go home.

FRE: (Still yelling, though now it appears the arms are back in a cartoonish type yell) Then go home! Why do you even work here?! No one wants you here!

At this point, there were still three of us out front waiting for our food. The team lead was managing the drive-through and trying his best to remain calm while helping his customers. He realized the three of us had heard everything. His eyes grew large as he told the two to take it outside.

The other customers and I looked at each other. The pregnant woman thought aloud, "I don't think I even want my food anymore. Just a refund would be great." I literally laughed out loud at her comment. I completely forgot that we ordered food. I was standing there, literally taking notes thinking, "I research this stuff! It's happening right in front of me!" The employees didn't hear her ask for a refund.

The event continued:

BE: (Still muttering and repeating her words. Calmly walks out the door stage right.)

FRE: (Still yelling, though now she's stomping through gathering her things.) I can't take this anymore! @#$#$@$#%! I hate this %$#@!%#$@! I need a smoke! (Storms out door, stage left)

Car doors slam, and a car peels out in the parking lot. The two in the argument are gone.

How much work do you think was getting done in that moment? Zero. Absolutely nothing. Why does nothing get done when conflict reaches high levels? Think about that answer as I continue with the story.

After she left, everyone was in a daze, trying to analyze what had just happened. About two minutes went by, when FRE walked back in! She came back in, calmer but still upset, grabbed something from the back-room area, mumbling the whole time, then left—passing two second-shift employees on her way out.

The second-shift employees cleared a path for her to leave, then looked at each other, went into the back room and asked what any of us would ask: "What in the world just happened?!"

The story is retold by a wonderful storyteller on first shift. It reminded me of how Michael Pena's character Luis tells stories in Marvel's *Ant Man* movie. It was very animated but slightly different from what had actually happened. The story retold by the first-shift employee, just a few minutes old, had already grown with embellishment. Remember, I was actually taking notes . . . like a nerd.

Just as the first shift employee is in the middle of his story, another second-shift employee came in and wanted to hear the story. The story-teller started the whole story over. The second-shift employee who had just heard the first half of the story had lots of questions and proceeded to interrogate the other first-shift employees while the story was being retold.

Then someone saw FRE in the parking lot trying to calm down. Now they're all looking at FRE wondering what she's going to do next.

There were four first-shift employees and two second-shift employees, and nothing was getting done. Even the team lead stopped serving the drive-through.

Long story short (there was more to the story. I just gave you the sweetened condensed version), it took us 25 minutes to get our food at a fast-food restaurant. People typically get antsy after two minutes at a fast-food place. Just yesterday at a fast-food location in Kentucky, I saw a man get his food within seconds! Twenty-five minutes is a long time. I felt terrible for the pregnant woman who was standing, being so patient. In the end, though, we got our food. I sat down to call the number to fill out a customer survey. I called the number and got an automated receptionist asking for a store number. Store numbers are supposed to be posted for this purpose. This store conveniently did not have their number posted, and I didn't think asking for it was a good idea at the moment.

When relational conflict was present, no work was getting done. Even after the two contenders left, the discussions kept going, and I have no doubt that the discussions continued for days after. Relational conflict causes problems that contaminate the water cooler. The stories spread and cause issues that decrease performance.

Relational conflict is the vacuum of success.

Relational conflict keeps leaders and managers up at night and makes them dread coming to work the next day. It's not even directly their problem, but they have to manage it because it's hurting the business.

Managing Relational Conflict in a Hyperconnected World

It is important to note how difficult it is for leaders to handle relational conflict in today's hyperconnected world.

Social media is tremendously influential in the world. It has brought forth many positive movements, but it has also been the cause of so much social destruction. People are armed with digital courage, saying things they would never say in person. When negative posts are created, they are often rewarded by receiving the approval of others via likes, shares and comments. Before social media, when a conflict would happen at work, employees could go home, reflect on the day and try again the next day. Now, in today's time of hyperconnectivity, when employees in the workplace engage in various forms of relational conflict, it can follow them everywhere they go as it rages on via social media.

Hyperconnectedness can not only bring work conflict home, but it can also cause external workplace conflicts to follow employees into work as well.[5] Relational conflicts and other such negative emotions originating outside of the workplace can still be devastating to workplace performance. It can be difficult as a leader to minimize relational conflict because as a leader, you are not just managing the person's behavior at work but managing all of their emotions as well because their negative emotions can affect your team success. Their emotions could have been stirred up by a great variety of things external to the team such as family, relationship, team, finance, health or social issues. In today's hyperconnected society, every aspect of our lives follows us everywhere we go.[6] We can be constantly reminded of all of our problems via our smartphones and emails, which can cause emotions to be raw even before an employee reaches the workplace. It is important that a leader handle these situations with care and understanding because as much as we'd like to say, "Hey, leave all of your troubles behind and work . . ." it doesn't always work like that. Just please be sensitive to the issues out there.

Relational conflict is not just the vacuum of success in teams. As previously stated, this applies to families, social movements, governments, parent–teacher organizations and universities. It applies everywhere. Relational conflict distracts from goals and strategy as well as decreases trust. It is a unity destroyer, which will be more evident as we discuss The Unity Formula. The good news is that relational conflict handled well can actually grow unity. Work to resolve relational conflict in your group, team or organization in a positive way that can, with time, actually make your team stronger.

Conflict is the last of the four components of unity. As we move forward, we will explore how to measure the four components of unity— and what to do with those measurements in The Unity Formula.

Notes

1. Suff, R. (2020, January). Managing conflict in the modern workplace | 2020 report. The Professional Body for HR and People Development. Retrieved from www.cipd.co.uk/
2. Inc., C. P. P. (2008, October 6). 2008 CPP global conflict report. Study Details Effects of Workplace Conflict on Businesses. Retrieved from https://shop.the-myersbriggs.com/PRESS/Workplace_Conflict_Study.aspx
3. Simons, T. L., & Peterson, R. S. (2000). Task conflict and relationship conflict in top management teams: The pivotal role of intragroup trust. *Journal of Applied Psychology*, 85(1), 102.
4. Cupach, W. R. (2000). Advancing understanding about relational conflict. *Journal of Social and Personal Relationships*, 17(4–5), 697–703.
5. Fredette, J., Marom, R., Steiner, K., & Witters, L. (2012). The promise and peril of hyperconnectivity for organizations and societies. *The Global Information Technology Report*, 2012, 113–119.
6. Sanz-Vergel, A. I., Rodríguez-Muñoz, A., & Nielsen, K. (2015). The thin line between work and home: The spillover and crossover of daily conflicts. *Journal of Occupational and Organizational Psychology*, 88(1), 1–18.

Part 3

Measuring Unity

Introducing the Focus, Direction, Trust and Conflict Scales

Maintaining unity is a struggle. Some days things are great. Other days are all over the place. The Unity Formula is a simple formula that was created as management tool to take a "snapshot in time" of unity in that moment. It is a measure of the team's potential that is being realized. A team member can apply the formula and get a feel for how things are and where attention can be focused to increase the team's unity—and increase the realization of the team's full potential of possibly becoming the next extraordinary team (ET).

As previously discussed, every team's unity exists on a scale. Unity is not an on/off switch. By measuring where a team member or entire team falls on the scale for each component—and later applying The Unity Formula—we can assess a team's unity and apply the right lure (remember the fishing ninja?) to help progress the unity of a team.

Seems odd to say, but through further research and application of the formula, not every team will reach a 10. Every team should aim for a score of a 10 in each of the four components understanding that even if you don't reach a 10, every team I've worked with, not most teams or a lot of teams, *every* team I've worked with that was committed to making a change was able to get all of their scores in the 6–9 range. Even if your team does not reach a 10 in *focus*, *direction* and *trust* (*conflict* is scored differently), you'll still notice tremendous improvements in unity moving from a 4 to a 6 or a 6 to an 8. The point is that the key to any team's improvement is to increase a team's unity and thus improve performance.

The lesson in using the scales is this: Shoot to be an ET but celebrate any improvement along the scale.

How the Scale Works

Each of the components of unity are broken down into a 1–10 scale. To help guide those using The Unity Formula, I've listed guideposts at scale points 1, 3, 5, 7 and 10 to help determine where your team may fit on

DOI: 10.4324/9781003269038-12

the scale. This means for each of those levels on the scale, I'll describe what someone who is at that level looks like in terms of their behavior, attitude and performance. As you read through, see if you can determine a number that appropriately applies to you or your team.

It is not intended that the guideposts provided at 1, 3, 5, 7 and 10 be the only numbers used. If the description at a guidepost fits perfectly, then use that number. But it is likely that you will find a team fits between two numbers. In this case, choose a scale point between two numbers. For example, if you find your team is a little bit more focused than a 1 but isn't quite to a 3, then you would choose a 2 for their focus.

As you read through the scale section, pick a team that you'd like to improve. Read through the pages with that team in mind, paying attention to how you would score that team and what you feel *the team's* overall score might be. Once each scale for *focus*, *direction trust*, and *conflict* are introduced and explained, then we will explore how to use the scale ratings in The Unity Formula—along with sharing applicable actions for improvement.

Chapter 7

The Focus Scale

As we explored in the previous section, focus is a measure of how intensely team members understand and commit to the goal. Focus is measured on a 1–10 scale, with 1 being the lowest level of focus and 10 being the highest.

Five guideposts for the focus scale are described next. Read these like they are statements that someone at this level could say to assess their level of focus.

1—What goal?
3—I don't know much about the goal. . . . I'm a really busy person
5—Okay, I am on board, but I have competing priorities
7—I'm all in, except when I'm busy, but when I'm here, I'm all in.
10—Laser-like focus on the goal, willing to sacrifice whatever it takes.

In determining a focus rating, there are two factors that may influence team members: external and internal. It's helpful to be aware of these factors as you consider the focus of your team.

External factors are commitments that influence focus. We operate in a hyperconnected society. We're not just connected to teams inside the workplace, but also outside the workplace. It is common to have an employee be a part of five to ten teams at the same time inside the workplace, all demanding time and energy. This leaves employees constantly triaging the wants and needs of each team to successfully be a member of all of them. This doesn't include the commitments outside the workplace. It's hard to keep focus on one goal when you're being pulled in 100 different directions. Now imagine a team of five each balancing their many commitments to other groups or teams while trying to stay committed to the goals of one team. External commitments can prevent team members from completely unifying.

Internal factors are a person's or team's beliefs about the goal. A person may simply not agree with the goal of the organization feel that the priorities are where they should be. This is a major problem. People often

DOI: 10.4324/9781003269038-13

quit their jobs over such misalignment. When a team member doesn't agree with a goal, the team member is less committed, their performance drops and they are more likely to seek out other employment.[1,2] Work becomes frustrating because the person truly believes the company is wasting their time.

As we explore the levels in the focus scale in this chapter, we'll cover what a person or team at that level may be experiencing externally and internally as they progress through the levels of the scale.

1—What Goal?

A person exhibiting a score of 1 in focus might be experiencing the following:

- *Externally*—A person or a team at a level 1 focus is not dedicating enough time to the goal to even give it a fair shot at success. They allow other priorities to take precedence.
- *Internally*—They're frustrated. Either they have no clue why they're heading in a direction, or they disagree with the direction they're heading. This can lead to backbiting, gossiping and providing just enough effort not to get fired.

Ever been a part of team where no one was really sure what was going on or why you were grouped together? What happens on that team? You've probably noticed everyone just does what they think they should do. The team isn't working toward anything. They're just doing, existing. This level of apathy about the goal is devastating for performance.

Despite the many books by many talented authors, there are still many groups that do not take the time to develop meaningful goals and make sure employees are committed to accomplishing the goals. In these groups, frequently the manager knows what the goal is, but the employees do not. The employees are mindlessly going through the motions, just following orders, without knowing why.

Groups like this are common in retail and manufacturing. Retail and manufacturing are environments where unified focus is often absent or barely present. These are industries with many metrics available, yet the metrics are rarely used by the people who can make the greatest impact. Instead, someone in the office sees the metrics and decides what should change to improve results. This information is passed through a chain of command, until it finally finds its way to team leads or supervisors in the form of a list of mind-numbing steps. No explanation, no discussion, no demonstration or painting of a vision—just a list of steps to be accomplished.

I understand the concept behind this form of management. When retail managers explain the reason for this form of management, it makes a little more sense. One of the first comments I hear from store managers is that numbers aren't shared, for example, because they don't trust their employees not to share these numbers with their competitors. I understand this concern. Turnover rates are generally higher in retail and manufacturing, with employees frequently switching between competitors. The managers' solution is not to share information with the lower level employees because they think odds are, the employees will probably end up leaving. This practice of not sharing is destructive to a unified focus. I see why managers may believe this, but there is a better way.

Another driver of this level of focus is when managers make a mix of statements that all blend together. Either they believe their employees aren't interested in the numbers or other business drivers, or they believe employees should first prove themselves at the lower levels, and then, if they're still interested, they'll be shown the numbers as they progress into leadership. After the employes work long hours; stand most the day; work nights, weekends and holidays, managers say they still want to see a little bit more commitment from their employees before they bring employees into the inner circle. This line of thinking is archaic. I know from my own experience owning a successful retail store that employees like knowing why decisions are made. I've found, in general, people are far more engaged in their work when they know why they're doing what they're doing. Author Simon Sinek wrote *Start with Why*.[3] I disagree with some of the concepts presented, but in general, I like the premise. Starting with why can build unity. More on this in the application section.

3—"Yeah, I'm Not Sure . . ."

A person with a score of three in focus might be experiencing the following:

- *Externally*—May show up to meetings but remain disengaged. They're interested in participating but are so busy that they only do the minimum to say they're involved.
- Internally—They may not agree with the goal of the team, but they'll move forward with it for now, as there is no better option. Or they might be actively seeking better options, but they'll stay here for now.

A hesitant participant is aware of the goal but hesitant to commit to it. A person at a 3 may be physically present but not mentally present. Probably on their phone a lot. This can be for a variety of reasons, but they all seem to be connected to the same excuse: "I'm busy." This is a common and very important excuse. If you're a great team member and known for success, then you'll probably be asked to participate on several teams. Still, a person needs to be judicious regarding the allocation of time.

This level is frequently found in nonprofits. People volunteer in non-profits for a variety of reasons. For some, it's because the nonprofit provided a service for them or their loved ones, so they feel the need to give back. For others, it's because a friend or a family member is volunteering there, so they thought it would be fun to volunteer as well. For some, it is to network. And still for others, it is because they feel the need to get out and do something. Whatever the reason, nonprofits love and appreciate their volunteers, though working with volunteers can be very frustrating.

Most volunteers "get it." They love the mission of the organization and want to be a part of the progress. But many volunteers are not fully committed to their role. The reason for this lackluster commitment is more common today than it used to be: We tend to overcommit. It comes from a good place, though. We want to do everything. We want our kids to do everything. We want to help everyone around us. On top of all of our team commitments, we still have to dedicate time to our relationships in order to keep them healthy as well. Many don't feel they have the time to do everything they would like to do. In 2019, volunteering hours were at their lowest point in decades despite a rising population.[4]

America's youth are experiencing a similar situation. On top of all the extra hours youth spend on school, sports, band or orchestra, working out, dance, cheer, theater, gymnastics, clubs, church groups, volunteering, gaming groups, etc., many are more involved scholastically than ever before. It is common to hear about students graduating with 30-plus college credit hours through taking Advanced Placement or dual enrollment classes. For many, their homework lasts long into the night; then they wake up early in the morning to repeat the process. I've heard numerous parents refer to themselves as a chauffeur or an Uber driver for their kids. I have no doubt that most of today's students love the busy experience, but the drain on the parents is exhausting.

In addition to our youth being busier, this makes the parents even busier. In today's hyperconnected society, we are constantly experiencing micro transitions, the transitions between roles that accompany every text, email, beep, ring or tweet. Employee micro transitions are a tremendous burden to both for-profit and nonprofit organizations.[5] One minute they are an employee or volunteer. Then they receive a message, and they transition to filling their role as a parent, friend, spouse or student—then back to volunteer, until the next interruption. It's okay, though, right? I mean, at least they're trying to help. At least they're part of the team. They're at the meetings. Unfortunately, people who choose to remain connected to all of their roles when trying to accomplish another role can be very distracting to others as well.

Overcommitment is tough to navigate because many choices are between good and better. This will be discussed later when we address suggestions for improvements.

Another factor contributing to being a 3 in focus is if a team member or a team is *allowing* themselves to be busy because they don't agree with the goal. You can be a great manager who inspires employees, shares information and details, brings everyone into the group and provides every belonging cue possible to all of your employees, but ultimately, if an employee doesn't want to be there or doesn't care, then they will "be busy" or remain uncommitted to the goal. This is a rough situation to be in because ultimately, if a person doesn't want to participate, they won't. Their focus will fall elsewhere.

Whatever the reason, a 3 in focus is the danger zone. Suggestions to improve focus and commitment can be found later in the book, but firing is not one of them except as a last resort. Working through rough times with employees increases retention, loyalty, determination, commitment and many other positive outcomes. Firing, while it has its uses, is a last resort in my opinion.

5—Okay, I Am on Board, But I Have Competing Priorities

A person scoring a 5 in focus might be experiencing the following:

- *Externally*—They have decided to commit time and energy to this goal. There are occasional distractions and competing conflicts, but overall, this person has decided that this cause is worth their time. They participate in meetings but keep their phones by their side to stay in touch with the outside world.
- *Internally*—They may not fully agree with the goal, but they're willing to move forward with it, as they feel it is a decent option. The commitment at this level is mixed. The goal and actions required to achieve it have to really appeal to the person for them to commit or dedicate any resources. They're interested, but they need to be sold a little bit more.

At this level of focus, a person has willingly joined the team because they believe in the mission and purpose, but they have higher priorities elsewhere. They may feel like they *need* to be on this team but don't really *want* to be a part of the team.

Most team members tend to fall into this category. As previously stated, we are hyperconnected. Not only are we part of multiple teams in and out of work, but all of these teams have access to us anywhere we have our phones. Each team requires time and energy. A person at a 5 has dedicated some of their time to a team but is constantly checking their phone and the time, ready to depart as soon as time is up. The person most likely puts very little time and effort into the project outside of the time spent together. Having said this, being a 5 isn't necessarily bad, but it's not the best.

7—I'm All in, Except When I'm Busy, But When I'm Here, I'm All in

A person scoring a 7 in focus might be experiencing the following:

- *Externally*—This person is attending and even contributing. They may or may not volunteer their time outside of the team meeting to continue working on the goals, but they are certainly moving things around in their schedule to ensure they can make things happen. This is a solid team performer—definitely a contributor.
- *Internally*—They agree with the goal. In fact, this person probably wishes they could devote even more time to the project. They are willing to sacrifice quite a bit for the goal but unable or unwilling to give it their all. They may even think about the project on their own time and work on the project a little outside of the team meetings, but it is unlikely.

The big difference with a level 7 is that while this person is busy, they tend to spend time and thought on the project even when the team is split up. A 7 in focus is a person who is committed as much as they can be at that time. They may even put their phone away during meetings, but they are unable to commit as intensely as a 10 might, though they probably wish they could.

I have found that most high-performing teams are focused at around a 6, 7 or 8. This is a great score. It's not an extraordinary team (ET), but it's still great! If every team in an organization were to be focused at these levels, the organization would have an excellent culture of teams and success.

I believe the reason most teams stop here is because

1. They don't know how to move beyond this point,
2. Current demands prevent the team from moving beyond this level, or
3. The amount of effort required to move beyond this point is large.

2 and 3 actually caused an issue with the early parts of my unity research. Initially, it seemed obvious that everyone should be at the highest level of each category to reach ET levels. If 10 is the best, why isn't everyone on a team striving to be a 10, right? But an employee who was a part of my research actually pointed out that her day-to-day job was filing documents at a doctor's office. She asked me why her team needed to be 100% unified all the time. I never thought of that before. Actually, you

don't need to be 100% unified all the time. It is quite useful when innovation, creation or drastic change is needed, but day-to-day operations certainly don't require a 10. Still, every team would benefit from being more unified.

10—Laser-like Focus on the Goal, Willing to Sacrifice Whatever It Takes

This is the ideal level of focus for a team or project. A person at a 10 is so focused that they may even forget to eat or call significant others. Other priorities take a backseat. This is their number one priority. Phones may be check or answered, but the message is the same: "I'm working on something. I'm going to have to call you back." When they do call back, they're rushing through the call to get back to work. When a group of people are at a level 10 focus together, they feel unstoppable. New discoveries are happening rapidly. A 10 in focus is often experienced in emergency situations, as discussed in the upcoming Findings section.

Take a moment and think about a team that you are on. Where would you or your team rank on focus using this 1–10 scale?

Notes

1. Vandenberghe, C., Bentein, K., & Stinglhamber, F. (2004). Affective commitment to the organization, supervisor, and work group: Antecedents and outcomes. *Journal of Vocational Behavior, 64*(1), 47–71.
2. Mercurio, Z. A. (2015). Affective commitment as a core essence of organizational commitment: An integrative literature review. *Human Resource Development Review, 14*(4), 389–414.
3. Sinek, S. (2009). *Start with why: How great leaders inspire everyone to take action.* Penguin.
4. Poon, L. (2019, September 11). Why Americans Stopped Volunteering. Bloomberg.com. www.bloomberg.com/news/articles/2019-09-12/america-has-a-post-9-11-volunteerism-slump
5. Ashforth, B. E., Kreiner, G. E., & Fugate, M. (2000). All in a day's work: Boundaries and micro role transitions. *Academy of Management Review, 25*(3), 472–491.

Chapter 8

The Direction Scale

If we were to score *direction*, the commitment to a plan or strategy, on a 1–10 scale, it might look something like this:

1—No idea what I'm supposed to be doing.
3—I think I know, but I'm unsure.
5—Okay. I'm pretty sure this is what I'm supposed to do.
7—Alright, we're getting stuff done. I get it now. . . .
10—Linked arms, skipping down the Yellow Brick Road.

1—No Idea What I'm Supposed to Be Doing

Not knowing what to do is a common feeling. It is actually very common to agree with an idea but never pursue it because pursuing it either seems too difficult or no one ever puts forth the energy to research and develop the strategy to accomplish the task. I think a lot of people forget that strategies sometimes require a lot of research and effort to develop. Thus, a lot of good ideas stop because no one really knows what to do.

I have a good friend who is an idea person. He comes up with ideas for everything. It doesn't matter what is going on; he can think of a better way of doing it . . . but my good friend struggles at his job. Again, he has all sorts of ideas on what could be better, but he isn't sure how to implement the solutions. He's an idea guy, not an implementor, not a doer. Many say identifying the correct problem is the key to success. Well, yes, that may be the key, but knowing how to fix that problem is the door handle that opens the door to improvement. That's why project management is one of the most desired trainings to have on a resume. Because it's evidence that you know how to get the job done.

What my friend is really good at, however, is identifying issues. This is a needed trait in the workplace. The act of identifying the processes that need to change is called deconstruction.

We engage in deconstruction all the time when we watch sports. We know exactly what's wrong with every play. To demonstrate our athletic

DOI: 10.4324/9781003269038-14

wisdom, we often make comments that are quite obvious to everyone watching the play. "Why didn't he pass to 88?! He was wide open!" "The 9-iron?! Of course you didn't hit the green. The wind blew it way off course!" "Should've seen the pick! #30 had a wide open three because he didn't see the pick!" It's easy for an armchair coach to give his advice based on replays. Everything is very obvious when we're far away from the action or watching a replay.

We can sit in an office, look at spreadsheets and say, "Why are we doing that? We need to change that." That's the focus part of unity—knowing the goal. Identifying what needs to be done and developing the plan to implement the change can be extremely difficult—especially when you're in the thick of an obstacle. That's when direction is needed.

Establishing strategy and direction setting is difficult and requires detailed planning and execution. The planning alone is often so difficult that many don't do it. They don't even put forth the effort to put the details in place to make goal achievement possible—leaving their team feeling lost and without a clue.

When at a 1 in direction, people aren't sure exactly what they're supposed to be doing. Someone, somewhere, may know exactly what everyone is supposed to do, but it hasn't been communicated, understood or developed yet. Team members are lost.

It is also possible that a 1 in direction also signals a resistance to the plan. For many reasons, someone may disagree with the path forward. Some common reasons are because they can think of a better path or because they don't understand how the strategy will reach success. It could be deeper: Maybe they don't even totally agree with the goal, and thus committing to a strategy is even more difficult.

The point is that a 1 in direction means that team members, whether by their own doing or by another means, are lost. They need to understand and increase commitment to the plan.

3—I Think I Know, But I'm Unsure . . .

Consider the repercussions of the statement, "I think I know what I'm supposed to do, but I'm unsure." Think of what you're willing to do when you are unsure versus when you are sure. For example, when you are following directions to a location, but you're not sure if you made a wrong turn or not: How do you feel? How does your behavior change? Most likely, you focus on the map more. You might turn down the radio to think more clearly. Maybe you even pull over to look at the map (hopefully not while you're driving), or worst-case scenario, you ask for directions, which, by the way, isn't as bad as TV shows make it seem.

These are common behaviors for people who fall at a 3 in direction. They move forward timidly, unsure if they're doing the right thing, not wanting to waste their time traveling down the wrong road.

This hesitancy is a major concern for players in one of the most famous reality shows of all time, *The Amazing Race*. *The Amazing Race* is a one-month race around the world, where the winners receive $1,000,000. Eleven to 12 pairs are chosen to compete. The pairs come from a wide variety of backgrounds. They have been married, dating, formerly dating—or are father and son, mother and daughter, brother and brother, brother and sister, sister and sister, coworkers, or best friends. The submission videos and questionnaires the network require from potential competitors allow information be revealed about a variety of subjects. Some topics include why they think they'd be great contestants, hobbies, backgrounds, what they would do with the winnings, food allergies, health concerns, etc. But one question that does not get asked is how good they are at using maps or following complex directions.

Navigating directions is crucial for every competing couple. At the start of each day, they are given a location to find their next clue. Seems like a simple assignment if you were looking in your hometown. But participants cover an average of 60,000 miles over the course of the race. Throughout the race, they find themselves in major English-speaking metropolises—and tiny, non–English-speaking developing country villages. Their clues take them to rivers, lakes, islands, small shops, bars, temples, restaurants, monuments, mountains and many other large and small destinations. Other than sometimes specifying a mode of transportation, the clues rarely provide any direction on how to reach their next destination. They must figure it out on their own.

Additionally, when they arrive at their location, they generally find a task waiting for them that must be completed before the next clue is given. Many times these tasks are location specific (small town in a distant country specific), are almost always unlike anything the racers have previously experienced and often involve a set of instructions that need to be followed exactly. Oh, and to add stress to an already stressful situation, the first to arrive at one of the 12 legs of the race first wins an additional prize, which could include cars, all-terrain vehicles, weeklong vacations and more. Getting to the end of each leg of the race first matters—which means getting lost or not knowing how to accomplish a task is devastating.

As a TV show that depends on building excitement to captivate the viewer, the editing team makes sure to highlight the poor decisions that couples make, giving their competitors a lead. In almost every leg of the race, someone gets lost or stuck on a task.

As a researcher, what I find interesting about those who get lost is what they do in those cases because it is extremely similar to what happens in the workplace. On the show, almost every team looks at another team's performance at some point to get a few clues on how to move forward, but those who are chronically unsure about their directions find themselves constantly relying on others. Often, teams that rely on others eventually find themselves lost without any other team to follow. This often causes confusion, stress and contention between the pair, which can increase the risk for additional poor decisions.

When we are unsure in the workplace or in life, we'll move forward timidly, ask someone for directions or just follow someone else. While asking or following others is good, ideally, we want everyone to feel confident in the direction they are heading. If a lack of confidence in a direction requires frequently asking others or following others, then the person will never excel because they'll constantly be behind everyone else. Additionally, learning is greatly diminished when a person is simply following someone else to the next step. It's like copying someone else's work on a project or copying the answers on a test. They may get the right answer in the short term, but in the long run, there will most likely be consequences.

Going in the wrong direction creates a terrible feeling. We want to achieve. We want to be successful. Feeling that we're not being effective or that we're lost brings emotions of defeat.

People want to know what they're doing is what they're supposed to be doing so they can do it well. When they are clear about what to do, they don't second guess themselves or timidly move forward, hoping not to move too far in the wrong direction. They go all in. They commit to their decisions.

The ideal situation is that everyone on the team knows exactly what they're doing and how to do it. This is important for two reasons. First, if everyone knows what they're doing and how to do it, then it frees up the leader to do what they need to do to support their team. Second, when a person knows they are doing the right thing, they can put their heart into it.

A solid sense of direction is needed for a team to be fully unified and become exceptional—reaching maximum potential. A team, working together, must commit fully to the goal *and* the plan to attain the goal. A person who is fully committed to the plan is an asset to the organization. They are able to give it their all because they know they are moving in the right direction. A 3 will struggle.

A team or a person who scores a level 3 on the direction scale will appear to be second guessing their efforts. They won't feel confident that they're doing the right things or moving in the right direction, so they won't put forth full effort for fear they will cause a problem. They may ask a lot of questions and seek reassurance. This is common for new people learning a new process, but it happens with more tenured people as well.

It's also important to point out that an employee at a 3 could also be a 3 because they're not committed to the strategy and thus they are performing poorly. They are purposefully putting forth limited effort because they don't want to go in that direction.

5—Okay. I'm Pretty Sure This Is What I'm Supposed to do

While still not following the plan in a truly unified manner, a team at a 5 in direction is starting to click. Some members may feel all-in. Some may not. Most are probably in the middle stage.

People at a level 5 in direction need affirmations. The need for affirmation isn't just a millennial or Gen Z thing, as many have suggested. It's a confidence thing. As previously discussed, we want to know that what we're doing is right.

At this stage, a common phrase one might ask here is, "Like this?" or "Is this what you mean?" This is a good sign. Many employees asking these questions want to excel but are just making sure this is what you want them to do. Many complained that millennials were constantly asking for approval from their supervisors. Here's a finding that may surprise some of you: After working with hundreds, if not thousands of millennials and their bosses, I've discovered that, general, millennials and Gen Zers are actually quite motivated, but they're not big on wasting time going down the wrong path (unless it's for social reasons; they're big on being social). Once they know the path is correct, they'll push forward with gusto.

Seeking constant approval could also be a sign of something worse, though. If employees are frequently seeking approval on seemingly every task they're given, it could be a sign of a negative management style we frequently refer to as *micro-managing*. Micro-managing is a term used to describe a manager who is so involved in every detail of a job that they often dictate not just the *what* but also the *how* of a task.[1] Micro-management is discussed further in the "Avoid Micro-management sec-tion toward the end of the book.

There are myriad events that could be occurring on a team that could be the cause for a 5 in direction. We have explored a few of them. Overall, when a team exhibits a 5 in direction, this can be a good sign indicating growth and potential commitment. But a chronic 5 in direction can be a sign that something is preventing full growth and development in unity.

7—Alright, We're Getting Stuff Done. I Get it Now. . . .

A team that is at 7 is really getting things done. With only a few exceptions, people are moving forward with their tasks and are committed to the plan that's in place. This creates a good feeling among team members. People know they're moving toward goal accomplishment. They're following the plan.

Similar to a 7 in focus, employees are starting to think about the strategy outside of work and may often arrive with a "Hey, I was thinking . . ." or may send after work texts saying "Hey, random question. What if we . . . ?" This is an excellent sign that team members are so committed to success that they're thinking about the project outside of the workplace. It feels good to know where you're going. People at a 7 feel confident in their direction and are thus able to suggest other ways to improve goal accomplishment.

Reaching this level marks a huge moment for a team. I know a 7 is not a 10, but a 7 or higher in direction is really quite an accomplishment to be proud of. Teams at this level are definitely performing.

At this high level of direction, however, there is a cautionary tale to tell.

A Cautionary Tale About High Levels of Direction

At a 7 in direction, people are putting their trust in the plan to accomplish the goal. They're following it closely and reporting back effectively.

It is important to know that as you move forward, it most likely will get harder before you reach your goal. It will be tempting for the leader to want to go back to the way things were. After all, things weren't that bad, right? At a 7 or higher in direction, people are very committed to following the plan. Therefore, the leader of the group cannot abandon their committed group without negative consequences.

You might be thinking, "Who would do that?" It happens more often than it should. As hundreds of employees have confirmed during our many sessions, though it's called many names and takes various forms, leader abandonment is one of the top reasons people are so resistant to change and commitment to new plans.

Here's a story to illustrate the frustration of a leader abandoning their team. See if it sounds familiar.

Imagine this. You're a team member at Best Pizza Co. You make good pizza, but it's not the best. It should definitely be better. The company would like to find a better way to make a pizza.

I use a mountain metaphor to discuss change in class. You are standing on top of a large mountain. It's not the best mountain in the world, but it's a good mountain. It's safe, comfortable and familiar. This is a good feeling.

Using the pizza example, all of the employees know how to make the pizza. Yes, it's not the most efficient way of making pizza, but it's good, and Best Pizza Co. does a pretty good job of selling pizza. It's got a decent following online. Yes, there are probably mountains with higher peaks and better views out there and maybe even better pizza, but this mountain peak is home, and the pizza isn't that bad.

Then a new person is hired to lead your store location. They start talking about how there are much better mountains out there, mountains with higher peaks and better views and—translated in this example—even better ways to make a more delicious pizza. This new person looks around and shows everyone how terrible the current mountain really is, things you really didn't notice before. The grass isn't as green as you thought it was here on this mountain, but on the other mountain, it is super green. You don't even have to wear shoes to walk on the green grass over there.

And the pizza?! The pizza almost makes itself, and it is so, so good.

Where does that leave you and the rest of the employees? You are now disgruntled with your current location and looking for a change. You don't know how to get there, but this new person claims he does, so you decide to follow him.

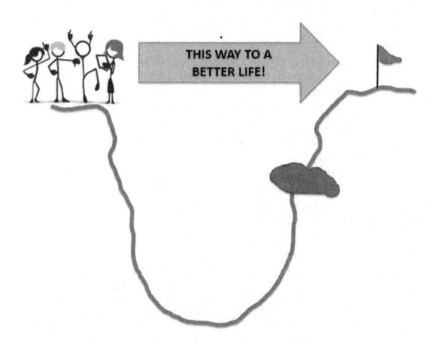

The journey begins with the descent down your mountain. Along the way, the new guy is pointing out every reason this was the wrong mountain, showing how the paths you had been following were inefficient. There were much better ways to get things done. All along the way, he is closing down those paths, pointing out how silly it was that you all had been making pizza like that for so long. He even mentions how lucky you all are to still be in business.

As the team descends down the mountain, they enter the *deconstruction* phase of change, identifying and stopping old habits to make room for the new ones. This stage of change does not take an expert, but there are plenty of people who believe that they are amazing leaders because they can point out everything wrong in the organization. That's not the difficult part.

Just because you can go in a restaurant and point out how it could be better doesn't mean you could run a restaurant. Deconstruction is both easy and hard. It is fairly easy to identify most problems. It can be difficult, however, to break old habits. Deconstruction is a very important phase, but it is not the most difficult. The challenge lies ahead. Back to the story. . . .

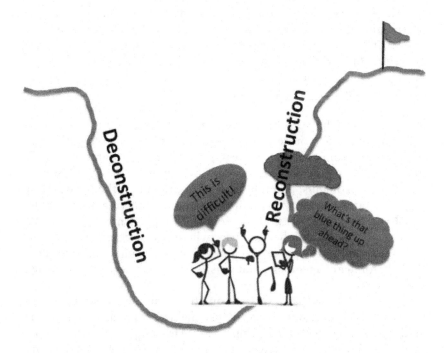

By this point, you are in the valley between the two mountains. You have stopped old habits and are looking forward to reaching this new peak with better processes, better pizza. All that's left now is the steep climb. No big deal, right? Who doesn't love a good challenge especially when pizza is involved?

This is where *direction* is put to the test. This steep climb toward the new peak is called the *reconstruction* phase, the phase when everything gets put back together. This is the phase when new processes and procedures are put into place. Commitment to goals and strategies are critical for this stage of change.

This phase requires patience and an open mind because new things fail all the time, but this doesn't mean the ideas are failures. It just means that the newness needs to be ironed out or maybe even washed out, but the process could still be good.

This is a difficult period to be in, though, because even though your team may see progress, the onlookers and doubters may not see it. Numbers may actually decrease at this point. You may even burn a few pizzas or get a few orders wrong. The team must continue to communicate both internally and externally to show successful progression toward the new summit.

Eventually, as you stick your plan, fully committed to following through on your path up the new mountain, you may reach what I call the "Pit of Despair." It is at this point that the team may view the task as insurmountable. When you started the deconstruction phase, it was easy to see that you needed to stop ineffective practices. When you started the reconstruction phase, it was easy to see that new practices needed to be put in place. But now that you are in the middle, many in your group are wondering if any of this was worth it.

You are caught in the Pit of Despair. New processes almost always have issues that have to be worked out. At this point in the reconstruction phase, as you're trying to put everything back together, all of the issues from the new processes are coming to light, and there are still more processes that need to be implemented. The team is stuck fixing problems, and they're getting tired of all the issues. Your customers and other pizza competitors are wondering what in the world you are doing, as nothing you have implemented seems to be working very well, and they can't see where you're going. They might even mock your attempts at reaching the new summit. It is extremely difficult for team members, but this is a crucial decision point for team leaders.

At this point, a leader may start to question if the new summit is worth it. I mean, the company was already making decent pizza. Why rock the boat? The customers weren't complaining. The company was getting by okay. How important is it to reach the new summit? All of a sudden team members and leaders may start to feel a lack of commitment toward the plan. They still want to achieve the goal, but this path is extremely difficult. Maybe someone could just order better ingredients to make a better pizza. One guy did that, and he was kinda successful. *Why is a complete reorganization needed*, right?

What would you do at this point? Hopefully, you would continue forward. If the research was done well, then the team should be confident that this new summit is worth the struggle. Trust your research! You're almost there. Push forward and make it happen. Most of you probably would.

Well, unfortunately, a lot of leaders are not like you all reading this book. Let me tell you what frequently happens in the workplace, causing employees to doubt new leaders and resist committing to strategic initiatives.

When the reconstruction gets tough, too many leaders abandon their teams at the Pit of Despair. The new guy that led the group here was tired of constantly defending his decisions. The stress of new processes failing and new ones still needing to be created was too much to handle. The increased pressure from upper management to deliver caused him to doubt how great the new summit really was. Fearing for his future, the leader, the one that's led you through the deconstruction phase and caused you to doubt the old way of doing business, now decides to take a helicopter ride back to the old familiar summit. Upon arrival, he calls to you all: "What are you doing over there? Get back over here! This place is nice! It's actually better than I thought."

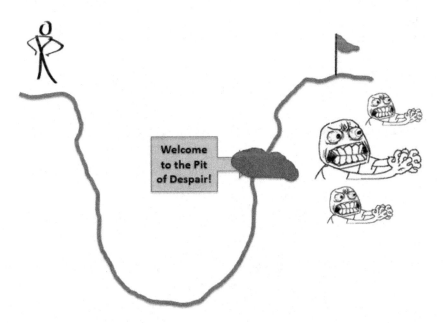

Your leader patiently waits for you to deconstruct all of the new processes you had been working on and reconstruct all of the old processes you spent so much time deconstructing. When asked what happened, he makes excuses and eventually stops talking about it. Things go back to the way they were. The pizza never tasted better . . . because you never did make it better. It's the same old pizza you've always made.

Eventually, the leader moves on to a new job somewhere else, leaving everyone else behind. People still question, "Whatever happened to . . . ?" You laugh, remembering crazy times. Then, one day, a new young leader shows up wearing new clothes and a bright smile. The new leader excitedly introduces himself as the person who's going to take you to new heights. He describes a new summit, a much better summit, and even shares stories of greener grass and incredible pizza.

Imagine your feelings. You probably wouldn't receive the new leader's vision very well.

Now imagine this had happened to you four or five times. How likely would you be to trust new leadership?

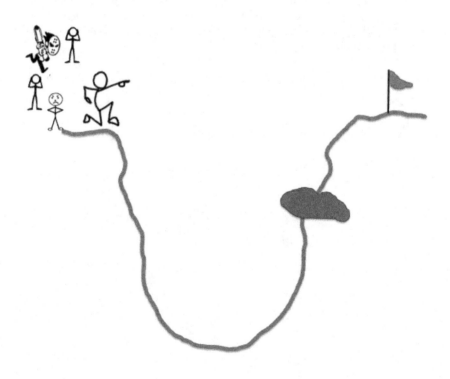

The issue with reaching a 7 or higher in direction is that team members have really bought into the direction in how to accomplish the goal. They are on board with the amount of work required. The team leader needs to follow through and take them all the way to the end; otherwise, it could have repercussions down the road for future leaders.

Once you reach a 7 in direction, the plan becomes extremely important because it is being followed by most of your team. Abandoning your plan may be necessary but do so cautiously. Things are really starting to click at a 7. Good work. Keep moving forward!

10—Linked Arms, Skipping Down the Yellow Brick Road

By this point, everyone is fully committed in following the plan to goal accomplishment. Being a 10 in direction, as with focus and trust, is extremely powerful. When a group is this committed to a plan, they'll move forward on their path regardless of dangers and peril. They're fully committed to making this work.

One of the most incredible feats of commitment to a plan was a religious migration west in 1846. Regardless of your belief on the religion, the migration demonstrated an inspirational example of how powerful a full committed group can be.

Brigham Young found himself to be the leader of a newly formed religious group that called themselves the Latter-Day Saints.[2] Believing to be called of God to lead this church, he went forth, helping the Saints get established and recover from the recent martyr of Joseph Smith, their founder. The Saints had been struggling to establish peace in their city of Nauvoo, Illinois, as they had in other locations. Mobs had assembled and were harassing the Saints, imprisoning their leaders, plundering their shops and homes and killing any who resisted. Brigham knew that they couldn't stay in the area much longer. The mobs were growing stronger and continued to push the Saints to leave. It was time to move.

Brigham had a dream. He dreamed that their new focus should be to move west to a new location. He wasn't exactly sure where the location would be, but he thought that it should be in the Utah/California area, which at the time was owned by Mexico. He believed the Saints would be safe in the mountains, away from persecuting groups. There, they would be able to establish life based on their beliefs and live in peace.

In a discussion with the Saints, he shared his plan to leave Nauvoo and walk over 1,000 miles to a new area far away from persecuting mobs, where he believed the Lord would protect them. His plan received mixed reviews.

For many, they were fully committed to the goal and to the plan. For them, this was *the way*—the direction or plan that they needed to follow. Thousands of members had lived through violent persecutions in Missouri and Ohio. Their goal was to establish Zion, a peaceful place where they could be unified in their worship of God. The new goal that Brigham presented seemed to many like an excellent idea. Moving far away to a land that was outside of the United States seemed like a great idea.

For some, however, this was the coward's way out. They believed there were plenty of other places much closer the Saints could move in order to have peace. They chose to stay. Some even left the church.

The ones that were focused and committed to the goal of establishing a new Zion in the West were in the thousands, but the problem was: how do you transport thousands of men, women and children over 1,000 miles across the Western frontier?

Railroad had yet to reach the West. There was a way to reach California by boat, but the Saints would have to travel down the Mississippi to New Orleans—or travel by land east to a port city on the East Coast. From there, they would have to take a ship around South America (Panama Canal wasn't completed until 1881) and back up the South American coast, until finally reaching San Francisco. Such a trip would be 13,000 miles, about four times the distance from England to New York and many times more treacherous. A trip by boat may have worked for a few people, but Brigham needed a plan for tens of thousands of Latter-Day Saints to reach the new city. Brigham decided it was going to have to be by land.

A journey across the Western United States by such a large group had yet to be accomplished. There were no official trails to follow. The cartographers of the day provided maps that were not as reliable as today's roadmaps. There were wild animals, lawlessness, poor shoes, limited food, rough terrain, illness, rivers to cross, weather to contend with and mountains to climb. The journey would require members to abandon most of their belongings, except what they could take with them in a wagon or by hand.

They would also have to be willing to start new lives. There was no village waiting for them, no food, no jobs, no homes and no buildings. Those who went were expected to build and contribute to the community and prepare a way for the other Saints to join them. In other words, Brigham was asking them to make an extremely difficult decision.

It was easy to commit to the goal. After years of terrible persecution from mobs, militia and the government, establishing a new city in a new land far from danger seemed great, but many bristled at the plan. Walking over 1000 miles, enduring months of extreme hardships with both old and young, giving up everything in their current lives and rebuilding all new homes and communities in a new, unfamiliar land was no easy plan to follow.

This would be a difficult choice for anyone, but those who decided to go believed it was the will of God and were fully committed to the plan, regardless of the hardships and trials. Those who embarked were "all in," fully committed to moving forward according to the plan Brigham had proposed.

After deciding on their new direction, the next few weeks were spent with the members selling their items and preparing for the journey. Because of the tremendous influx of properties and products on the market, the Saints were offered very little for their belongings. Some barely had enough to purchase the necessary supplies for the long journey Many didn't have enough to cover all of the expenses and relied on the kindness of others.

In the end, 1,600 people had signed up to be the first group to cross the plains. They didn't know how they were going to make it. They didn't even know exactly where they were going. But they knew that it was the plan, so they sacrificed everything to push forward. The terrain was rough. The inexperience was obvious. The weather was uncooperative. Their supplies were lacking. Illnesses tested faith. Deaths broke hearts, but despite many opportunities to quit, turn back or join a neighboring town, they pushed forward fully committed to the plan to walk to their new home, of which they had little clue where that was to be.

Over the next 20 years, more than 60,000 Latter-Day Saints traveled to Utah following the same Mormon Pioneer Trail. Thousands were from other countries that had traveled by ship to the United States and walked the many miles without any belongings, enduring more than six months of travel. Many pioneers kept track of their accounts in their journals, providing today's historians with countless stories of struggle, weakness, doubts and even death, but their accounts also spoke of great hope, commitment and dedication.

Eventually, the Transcontinental Railroad was completed in 1869 with a stop in Salt Lake City, providing safer, faster passage. Before the railroad was completed, Latter-day Saints around the world knew that if their goal was to reach Salt Lake City, they would have to be fully committed to the plan.

A 10 in direction is extremely powerful. If people believe in the plan, they'll overcome the unknown. They'll be willing to face uncertainty. They'll figure it out. They'll work the long hours. They'll sacrifice what they need to sacrifice. They will get the job done.

Notes

1. Wigert, B., & Pendell, R. (2021, September 13). The ultimate guide to micromanagers: Signs, causes, solutions. Gallup.com. www.gallup.com/workplace/315530/ultimate-guide-micromanagers-signs-causes-solutions.aspx
2. Latter-day Saints, T. C. of J. C. of. (2020). *Saints: The story of the Church of Jesus Christ in the Latter Days* (1st ed., Vol. 2). The Church of Jesus Christ of Latter-day Saints.

Chapter 9

The Trust Scale

Of all four unity components, trust is the most difficult to break down and define (and thus measure) because trust can take many different forms—and a lack of trust can bring various consequences.

It took years for me to define trust in a way I feel comfortable with. One of the reasons why it took so long was because I truly believed that if unity was as powerful as I claimed that it was, then its components must be applied similarly in every scenario. I'd witness something on a sports team and write it down. Then I'd go to a retail team and discover something different but similar. Then a healthcare team would be totally different all together.

Eventually, though, as Jeff Foxworthy humorously quips, "It was in the last place I looked." Once it hit me how trust fit into unity, it's been fun seeing it all play out.

The trust I'm referring to as one of the key components of unity is *social trust*, as I've shared.

I recognize, as described earlier, that *physical* trust is crucial. *Performance trust*—or trust in the performance of your teammates—is also necessary. But these two trusts are fairly well understood. It's kind of a given that you need to trust that someone isn't going to steal from you or that everyone on the team is actually going to work.

I guess what I'm saying is that there is a caveat to this component within The Unity Formula. As long as the minimum requirements are met for physical and performance trust, then the most important trust to take a team to the extraordinary level is social trust.

There are various levels of social trust. This is the component where I hear the most "That's totally my team right now . . ." type statements. Hopefully when you recognize your team, it will be on the higher end of the scale. Let's explore/ . . . As you read, consider where you or your team falls on this scale.

DOI: 10.4324/9781003269038-15

1—No One Talks

This is a classic scenario. Boss enters the room, says her/his announcements, asks for feedback, none is given, then everyone leaves. Very little discussion occurs outside of the board room, and very little feedback, positive or negative, happens among the team.

An individual at this level is a very self-centered member of the team. They look out for themselves.

A team this low in trust is often very temporary, requiring very little interaction—or is governed by fear. Not necessarily fear of physical harm or losing their jobs but social fear. They don't want to look ill-informed or incompetent in front of their colleagues. Members may be afraid to speak up. They only do what they're told to do, no more, no less. If they do more, they might get it wrong and get into trouble. If they do less, they will definitely get into trouble. This is a tough scenario to be in.

Some scenarios influencing trust levels are only temporary. A strong disagreement may have occurred just minutes before, when some things were said that should not have been said. Trust might be temporarily damaged but can be resolved with time—assuming the pattern does not repeat itself often.

A chronic lack of trust at this level will result in a high turnover rate in a good job market. If the job market is poor and employees are stuck where they are, then you'll get very little extra effort from them.

Some research actually mentions that this stage of trust occurs in any new team.[1] Not necessarily. When a new team forms, people join the team and bring with them their "new team" stereotypes. Some may wonder if the team will be successful. Others may be trying to decide what role they will play: *Who will play the clown? The loafer? The leader?*[2] Some might even show up ready to get started. The point is that the discomfort inherent within a new team and new situation is not necessarily related to a lack of trust.

I'm not sure where this originated, but I've heard it repeated several times that some interviewers can tell within a few minutes if a person can be trusted and will be a good fit on a team. Elon Musk recently mentioned it in an interview.[3]

Trust can be formed very quickly. For example, Lord Shackleton's team to the South Pole was created with just five-minute interviews. Some of this instinct to trust comes from previous experiences meeting new people or being in new groups. Positive experiences with others in teams tends to increase the chances that members will place trust in their new teams. A person with negative experiences in previous teams tends to act distant and less willing to jump into team-building exercises. People approach new teams based on previous experiences, but the speed at which trust grows on a new team can be rapid. Those initial interactions in the first five minutes have a big impact on how quickly trust is built.

3—Some Sharing But Not in a Group

A group at a level 3 in trust is likely not to share ideas, opinions or feedback in the group, but they do so may outside of the group. At this level, the team may be splintered into two- to three-person groups that are cohesive outside of the team. The mini-groups may sit together, joke together and even eat lunch together, but they are not likely willing to include others in their subgroup. They're untrusting of the others.

Groups like this often include competitive people who appear to be vying for a top spot in the team. Competition can be great if everyone believes the competition is fair and if the team is competing against another team. If it is perceived to be unfair or if there's competition within the team, then it creates tension (and often conflict). This type of competition is common at a measurement of 3 in trust.

5—Sharing But Timid About Sharing

At this point, the team is starting to gel. Those who may feel uncomfortable about sharing may start sharing timidly. There may still be cliques. Often there are people on the team who are not exerting effort to build the team trust; therefore, they come off as aloof and disrupt the psychological safety of the team. It's hard to trust someone that appears as if they don't want to be there.

7—More Open Communication; It's Getting Louder

Now we're talking—literally! Groups are talking and giving each other feedback, celebrating wins, and talking about losses. They're starting to joke around with each other.

It's interesting to me how humor often accompanies higher levels of social trust. Humor is discussed in more detail in an upcoming chapter, but humor both builds and reinforces social trust. One author quipped:

> In workplaces that encourage people to be themselves—that are less hierarchical and more innovative—people tend to be more open with their humor. . . . Even people who aren't always comfortable sharing their humor tend to do so in more relaxed environments where the use of humor becomes second nature with everyone's style.[4]

You'll definitely notice at this level social guards are coming down and good times are increasing. People are feeling more socially comfortable and thus more humorous. It's not necessarily like a party, but it is people having a good time pursuing the goal, which is a great thing to have.

If your team is at a 7, good work! Keep it up. Trust grows trust. As long as positive experiences are allowed to happen, you'll most likely be at a 10 soon.

10—Open Sharing of Ideas, Family-Like

I opened the book by talking about how you know a good team when you see one. Well, that's how it is at a 10 in social trust. You just know it. Everyone is clicking. Every member is comfortable being themselves. They're laughing, bringing food and picking on each other in a loving, friendly-type way. They share ideas freely and aren't afraid to correct each other because they trust the other person isn't trying to be cause harm. They spend time with each other outside of work—either in person or by other means such as texts, phone or social media. They enjoy being with their team members.

It's been stated a few times that you don't *need* social trust to accomplish a goal, but on top of all the other numerous benefits of social trust, when a team reaches a 10 in social trust, it's just more fun.

Notes

1. Tuckman, B. W., & Jensen, M. A. C. (1977). Stages of small-group development revisited. *Group & Organization Studies*, 2(4), 419–427.
2. Driskell, T., Driskell, J. E., Burke, C. S., & Salas, E. (2017). Team roles: A review and integration. *Small Group Research*, 48, 482–511.
3. Popomaronis, T. (2021, January 27). Elon Musk asks this question at every interview to spot a liar-why science says it actually works. CNBC. Retrieved from www.cnbc.com/2021/01/26/elon-musk-favorite-job-interview-question-to-ask-to-spot-a-liar-science-says-it-actually-works.html
4. Kerr, M. (2015). *The humor advantage: Why some businesses are laughing all the way to the bank.* Michael Kerr.

Chapter 10

The Conflict Scale

Conflict is different than the previously described keys. The other three are very positive, unity-building numbers you'd like to increase. For conflict, this is a number you'd like to decrease. It is the vacuum of success, the destroyer of unity. Manage conflict and keep it at a 1. The formula introduced earlier and explained later reflects the detrimental nature of conflict.

During one of my trainings, a person stopped me at the break and asked the following:

ATTENDEE: This doesn't seem fair. The potential of my team is more than cut in half because my conflict is at a 3.

JOHN ROSS: What's unfair about that?

ATTENDEE: The team has all of these other good things about it, but just because two people don't get along, then it could hurt the team this badly?

JOHN ROSS: Absolutely. Relational conflict is *that* bad.

ATTENDEE: (incredulously) So just because some people are in a room gossiping about other members of the team, it can hurt the team that badly?

JOHN ROSS: Definitely. Absolutely.

I then proceeded to explain why relational conflict hurts the team so much. I explained the 25% rule (explained later). Two people in a team of 50 might not matter as much, but two people in a team of six, as was her team, mattered a big deal. Upon further reflection, as we talked about their behaviors and her teams reactions to the two involved in conflict, that those people who were causing conflict were holding her team back from so much more positive potential.

As you read through the conflict scale, use your best judgement where your team might be. And keep in mind that while your team may be high in conflict at this moment, conflict can be resolved in a positive way,

DOI: 10.4324/9781003269038-16

helping all parties involved to grow, but at the moment in time that relational conflict is present, it is detrimental to team unity.

1—Virtually No Relational Conflict

This is a great place to be. Everyone is working together, putting aside differences and making stuff happen. Not much to say about this. It feels good to be at this point.

2—Silent Conflict

Many people think that just because conflict isn't visible, then everything must be good. This is absolutely not true.

This is where trouble begins. Silent conflict is when someone doesn't like someone else. They're not saying anything about it, but they're also not overlooking it. They're continuing to work while holding a grudge against another person. This can last for many days or weeks. I knew one team in which silent conflict lasted over a year!

This is definitely better than gossiping and backbiting (a 3), but it is not helpful to the grudge holder. It eats away at them, and if not resolved, can result in outbursts of pent-up, negative energy.

People may result to a variety of coping mechanisms because they feel powerless and think that if they stay quiet long enough, then the problem will go away. This can be true, but too often, it does not go away—meaning if this conflict doesn't get worked out, it affects the team even more.

The way it affects the team can be numerous, but the main one is that people start to withhold information from each other. If person A does not like person B, then person A might not share information that could potentially help person B. If person B does not receive that information, then it makes it more difficult for that person to excel—which hurts the whole group. Person A might actually try to avoid person B and possibly even refuse to work with person B even if it may benefit the team.

It is important to understand that a team can only reach its full potential when everyone is working together in unity. Harboring harsh feelings is not good for any team and hurts team success.

It is important to note that many teams I have worked with talked about being professional. You can disagree with a person and still work with them. You can put aside differences and make work happen. A person or team only moves up on the conflict scale if the conflict is causing harm to the team.

I've worked with several performing arts groups with great success. When you have a performing group with dozens of people, there's an excellent chance someone in the group has relational conflict at some point with someone else in the group. However, realizing that the goal is to put on an amazing performance, the two could decide to put aside their differences and their grievances with each other and make the performance as excellent as it should be. In a case like this, if conflict is not preventing two people from sharing information, is not causing the withholding of information or feedback, gossiping, backbiting or physical altercations, then I'd say the team members are being professional about it and that their rating should probably remain at a 1. Monitor such relationships, though, because we have all had unprofessional moments.

3—Backbiting and Gossiping

Gossiping and backbiting occur when a person doesn't like someone, and they have to let everyone know about it by hurting their reputation and status in an organization. The late Chinese general Sun Tzu in his book *The Art of War* would refer to this as "informal" war, meaning this is the battle without weapons.[1] It is an extremely effective form of warfare—so effective that Sun Tzu actually mentions several times that a battle can be won even before it is fought, through an effective, informal campaign.

This is the goal of gossiping and backbiting—to take down a person without actually having to face the person.

The root of gossiping and backbiting is pride. Pride is demonstrated as self-centeredness, conceit, boastfulness, arrogance or haughtiness. Essentially, pride is the trait that opposes others. In the words of C. S. Lewis: "Pride gets no pleasure out of having something, only out of having more of it than the next man. . . . . It is the comparison that makes you proud: the pleasure of being above the rest. Once the element of competition has gone, pride has gone".[2]

Competition can be great to motivate a team, but when feelings of anger toward another continue beyond the healthy competition, that is pride. This is not team pride that I refer to, in which the team unites under a common banner to compete against a common competitor. This is personal pride, an anger or hatred toward others. Such pride does *not* motivate a team.

The opposite of pride is humility. Humility is when you can look at yourself and realize you still have a lot to learn. Humility is not a sign of weakness. Humility is at the core of learning. You must humble yourself enough to realize that you are good at what you do, but you could be better. Humility is okay to have when others outperform you. It doesn't mean that you don't try your hardest to win, but if someone else wins, there's a respect for that person and their abilities, not jealousy and annoyance.

Humility is inward focused, looking to improve oneself. Pride is outward focused, looking to outperform everyone else. Humility wants to build oneself and other up.

Humility enjoys the game. Pride only enjoys domination over an opponent.

Gossiping and backbiting are attempts to destroy unity. They make someone or something look better by making everyone or everything else look worse.

A good friend once told me that there are two ways to have the tallest tower: You can either work hard and build a strong, tall tower, or you can knock down everyone else's tower. Pride seeks to both build the tallest town and to knock down everyone else's tower instead of appreciating the urban beauty of many tall towers together.

Pride is devastating for team performance because it distracts people from the goal and plan. It destroys trust. A person's focus changes from the team goal that everyone is committed to into just being the number one person on the team.

Gossip and backbiting can spread like a disease throughout an organization, especially with social media. It can hurt relationships by spreading false narratives.

If you find your team is a 3 in conflict, the situation needs to be improved quickly.

5—Physical Altercation

Conflict, at times, gets so intense that a fight breaks out. This destroys productivity in the moment, and for a long period of time after, productivity plummets. Everyone wants to know what happened, and everyone has a different opinion on who should've done what and why. Unity is gone. Productivity is virtually gone. No work is getting accomplished. The goal has changed from working together as a team to everyone trying to compare information to create an accurate story of what happened.

I have seen many examples of a 5 in conflict being improved to a much better score, but if you find your team has a 5 in conflict, expect a few days or longer of getting everyone refocused on the goals and strategy—and rebuilding social trust.

Notes

1. Tzu, S. (2006). *The art of war*. Filiquarian Pub.
2. Lewis, C. S. (1952). *Mere christianity*. Macmillan, pp. 109–10.

Part 4

The Unity Formula

Introducing The Unity Formula

The Unity Formula is a tool that was created for team leaders/members to use to help manage their teams. It measures a snapshot in time. A team's unity could be good one day and poor the next, but an extraordinary team tends to have high scores most of the time.

Besides providing an overall unity score, this diagnostic tool can help identify the problem area, so the appropriate solutions can be applied.

Following the step-by-step instructions in the upcoming pages, the previously identified points from the previous chapters on the focus, direction, trust and conflict scales will be inserted into the formula in the appropriate areas. The first step of the formula will provide your team score. The second step consists of you comparing that score to the score of a perfectly unified team, which will give you a percentage of unity. This percentage will help you identify the team's potential that you are currently realizing versus what remains untapped. Key formula findings and suggestions for improvements will follow.

DOI: 10.4324/9781003269038-17

Chapter 11

Applying The Unity Formula

Now it is time for you to apply The Unity Formula. First, let's revisit the equation to determine your team unity score, and then we will step through a hypothetical example before letting you practice with your own scores.

$$\text{Your Team Score} = \frac{((\text{Focus} \times \text{Direction}) + 2 \times \text{Trust})}{\text{Conflict}}$$

Step 1: Insert Your Four Scale Points and Solve

The first step is to insert scale points assigned to focus, direction, trust and conflict at the appropriate points indicated in the formula above. Then solve.

Here's an example.

Company: Average Widget Productions
Company Motto: "We're not the best, but we're pretty darn good."

Widget Production Team Unity Score: Focus: 6; Direction: 6; Trust: 8; Conflict: 1

Step A

Let's tackle the first part of the problem. In the formula, the crucial, hope-bearing first step is Focus × Direction. Insert the scores provided by our Widget Production Team. Focus and Direction were both a 6. Therefore:

Multiply focus times direction: Focus × Direction = 6 × 6 = 36

DOI: 10.4324/9781003269038-18

Step B

Step B adds trust into the equation. We have our first score of 36 from multiplying Focus and Direction in Step A. Now add the insert the Trust score (8) into the formula and continue solving:

2 × Trust = 16

Put the entire top half of the equation together:

Focus × Direction = 36 (from step A)

2 × Trust = 16 16 (from step B)

36 + 16 = 52. This is our top half of the equation, or our numerator.

Step C

Now for the relational conflict score, or in the equation, our denominator. It looks like the team from The Average Widget Production company got along great. I'm sure they disagreed from time to time, but nothing was taken personally. They had an extremely low conflict score of 1. Therefore:

(Focus x Direction) = 36 (step A) + (2 × Trust) = 16 (Step B) = 52

Conflict = 1

Any number divided by 1 is the same number. So . . .

52 (Focus × Direction + 2 × Trust)/1 (Conflict) = 52

52 is the team score for Average Widget Productions.

Step 2: Compare Your Team's Score With the Perfect Score

Next, the team score is added into the second part of the formula to learn what percentage of a team's potential is actually realized. Think of this as movie reviews on such movie review sites as IMDB or Rotten Tomatoes. Movies on these sites are given a percentage based on critics and audience scores. A 10 on IMDB is a perfect score. Rotten Tomatoes' high score is 100%. Based on how close a movie's score is to a perfect score, you have a pretty good idea if a movie is one you might enjoy or not.

This portion of the formula compares a team to a perfect extraordinary team (ET). Following this portion of the formula will give you a percentage. This percentage will help you determine how unified a team really is and, consequently, if you might enjoy being on a team as unified as the score indicates.

The Average Widget Production team has a team score of 52.

The total possible score is 120. This is found by inserting the best scores for each of the components in The Unity Formula.

The calculation for total possible score:

10 in Focus, 10 in Direction, 10 in Trust, 1 in Conflict
10 in Focus × 10 in Direction = 100 +
2 × 10 in Trust = 20.
100 + 20 = 120
120/1 in Conflict = 120. This is the perfect score.

Continuing our example above with Average Widget Productions:

Team score: 52
Total possible score: 120
Team score/Total possible score = 52/120 = 43.33%

This is a total of 43.33% of unity achieved, or 43% of total team potential being realized. Based on what I've seen, this isn't bad at all. As I'll explain later, this is an above-average team. There's plenty of room for improvement, but so far, this team is on the right track.

Formula Practice

Now it's your turn to practice using the formula. As I mentioned in the scales section, you can choose any team to analyze. It may be useful to use a team that you are currently on. I recommend you choose a team you are familiar with.

Once you have chosen your team, look back on the focus, direction, trust and conflict scales and decide where you think this team would fall on each of the scales. Then, using the space provided, practice using the scale.

Team Name: _____

(If this is a book that will be shared, you might not want to list the name of a specific team that someone else may recognize. Feel free to use Widget Company.)

Scale Points:

Focus: _____
Direction: _____

Trust: _____
Conflict: _____

Unity Formula:

Focus _____ × Direction _____ = _____

_____

2 × Trust = _____

Focus × Direction _____ + 2 × Trust _____ = _____

Combined score from above:

(Focus × Direction + 2 × Trust) _____/Conflict

_____ = _____ Team score

Now for part two of the formula:

Your team score _____/Total possible
score __120__ = _____%

This number represents your percentage of unity, or the amount of your team's potential that you are realizing. Remember the score. In the upcoming chapters, I discuss which percentages are in the below average, average, above average, and ET ranges along with additional findings while using the formula.

Before moving on from The Unity Formula, however, I recommend scoring a few more teams. Once you get the hang of it, you'll probably be able to get a good estimate of a team within a minute or two.

Teams using this formula tend to fall in one of five categories. The categories are briefly described below:

1. **1%–19%**—Low-performing teams (as determined by team members and management). These poor teams are missing out on 80% or more of their potential! These teams are often riddled with problems and conflict.
2. **20%–40%**—Average teams. Most teams fall in this category. I've had one person mention that this didn't make sense to her. Wouldn't average be 50%? Well, no. Would you watch a movie that was 50% on Rotten Tomatoes or visit a restaurant that was 2.5 stars on Google or Yelp? Probably not. We have standards. Average is not always right in the middle.
3. **41%–70%**—High-performing teams. This is a broad range, but teams in this category share similar traits and performance. They are great teams to be a part of. As previously stated in the earlier

chapters, even if your team never makes it to an ET but *does* make it to this level, you should consider that a victory! There is more work to be done, but this is a great team. This is about the level that relational conflict is almost nonexistent. That's how damaging relational conflict is to a team. The existence of it will make it extremely difficult to move beyond an average team.

4.   71%–89%—Teams at this level are extremely similar to ETs and may even have been an ET earlier in the project. A few slight adjustments and increases in unity, and this team is an ET.

5.   90%–100%—ET

Frequently Asked Questions Regarding

The Unity Formula

In addition to unique and interesting findings, as I'll share in the upcoming chapters, I have also witnessed a trend in the questions asked about The Unity Formula. Questions or doubts can hinder knowledge acquisition, so I hope to address some of those questions in this section before we move on. This chapter explores some of those questions—and their answers.

This Formula Is Very Subjective. Is This a Problem?

It depends on how you are using the formula. As a quick tool, it is, in my opinion and in the opinion of many who I work with, the best tool for a quick evaluation of a team's unity. If you're looking for an objective measure, yes, I do have a questionnaire that is filled out, analyzed and then reported back (by me) to the leader with suggestions for improvement. This is part of the consulting that I do, which is what led to a lot of the information in this book. This will help take out some of the subjectivity of "diagnosing" your own team. I have been able to diagnose a team many times without meeting them, simply by applying The Unity Formula based on the questionnaires filled out by team members. I generally do not recommend this because I am a firm believer that quantitative measures are only symptoms of reality. Qualitative follow-up should occur for a clearer picture of the situation.

Even though the usual method of using the formula alone, without outside guidance, is very subjective given that it is filled out by someone close to the team without additional oversight, I've found that the leader normally has a gut feeling about how things are going. They seem to be pretty in tune to the unity.

Why Is Trust Separated Out Like It Is? Shouldn't It Be (F × D × T)/Conflict?

Good question. Based on my research, trust is really only required for the highest, ETs. I've been on several groups and teams as a team member where we were just doing day-to-day tasks that didn't require a lot of innovative interaction. We were just doing our parts. That's it. Thus, the most important factors in unity are focus and direction. When extraordinary creativity and innovation are required, then trust is needed to get to that "magic" level.

The Entire Formula Is Divided by Relational Conflict? That Seems a Little Harsh. Even the Small Stuff Is That Bad?

Yes, relational conflict is that harsh. It absolutely impacts focus, direction and trust in a dramatic way. What would happen to productivity in the workplace if a fist fight were to occur? Even if the offenders were escorted off premises, would everything return to normal? No way! Everyone would be discussing the fight! There would be rumors, upset feelings, taking sides, management guidance. Even a seemingly small relational conflict can cause major issues. Backbiting, gossiping and withholding information are just a few extremely negative consequences that come from relational conflict.

Just to show a very near, real-world example, we recently let someone go from one of our electronic stores because she was toxic. One by one, she caused a problem with each person in the store. We normally have a very unified team, but with her in our company, our unity was fractured. We regularly pay for group outings and such, but no one wanted to attend if she was there. Generally, I do not agree with firing. I think most people are worth time in keeping. Having said this, I also understand that some people continue to be toxic to the organization despite investing time and resources. Therefore, after several rounds of coaching and a few incidences, we let her go. The mood improved immediately.

Relational conflict is extremely damaging to culture, performance, and of course, unity. Reed Hastings, long time chief executive officer of Netflix, is big on removing toxic employees from the workplace quickly. He pays a severance, thanks them for their service and then lets them go. He has said many times that it just isn't worth it to retain toxic employees.[1] Relational conflict is rough.

It Seems That a Change in Score to One of the Components Would Change the Others as Well. Is That Intentional?

This is true for most any related terms in research. The composition of unity includes an extremely interwoven web of relationships. A small adjustment in one area could greatly improve another area. For example, two people may not like each other because they do not know each other. Reducing relational conflict could also help these two people adopt the goal more intensely (focus), work together better (direction) and increase trust. Instituting a successful communications campaign could help build focus and direction but not social trust among the team. The components are definitely related but can be influenced separately.

This Is a Pretty Simple Idea . . . The Workplace Is More Complex Than This, Right?

I have found that generally the best ideas are often the simplest. The workplace is complex, but diagnosing and resolving a problem can be simple. This is especially clear in process improvement initiatives.

I'm a Lean/Six Sigma Black Belt. That means I've passed the training, tests and projects to acquire a high rank in the process improvement discipline. I've led many projects and been a part of many more. One of the key principles of Lean/Six Sigma is to look for the simple answer because sometimes, that's all it takes.

One of my favorite examples happened to a friend of mine. He was called in because an area was experiencing many problems. People were calling in sick. Production was down. People dreaded working in this one particular area. My friend went over and did his initial study to investigate the problem. During his investigation, he discovered that the #1 reason people were calling in sick was because of back pain. Long story short, the table they were working at was about nine inches too short for the height of the employees. Here's the kicker: They were adjustable tables! Anyone could have applied the solution had they known the correct problem to fix. The tables were adjusted, and production improved overnight.[2]

The Unity Formula helps team leads, members and managers identify where their team is lacking so the appropriate solutions can be applied. Often, the solutions are extremely simple to implement. One of the most common solutions to problems in the workplace is communication. We are still explaining to students and professionals the importance of talking to one another, communicating ideas and disagreements. Training people to talk to each other, not at each other, is a multimillion-dollar industry. It doesn't get more basic than that.

Simple does not equal ineffective. The formula is simple, easy to remember and absolutely quickly applicable. Simplicity is one of its strengths!

Notes

1. Charan, R. (2019, January 10). How Netflix Reinvented HR. *Harvard Business Review*. hbr.org/2014/01/how-netflix-reinvented-hr.
2. Ross, J. (2012, August 15). Lean/six sigma master black belt shares story on simple solutions.

Part 5

Increasing Unity

Introduction to Increasing Your Team's Unity

Now that you've been introduced to the four keys of unity, seen The Unity Formula, learned how it works and assessed your team to determine opportunities for improvement, it's time to shift our focus to how to increase unity with the teams in your life. As I've mentioned, improving your score even slightly can make vast differences in your team's unity and performance. So, even if your team never makes it to being an extraordinary team, any improvement in unity will be noticeable.

No matter the team you're attempting to improve, whether it be a family, sales, sports, retail, spouse or partner, friends, healthcare, etc., these suggestions are for you. It is important to note that these are suggestions. Without knowing your specific situation, it is difficult to prescribe the exact fix to your problem. But hopefully there are at least a few suggestions that stick out as possible solutions to organizational unity problems. The next book will highlight many more suggestions with much greater detail, but I wanted to leave you with at least a few suggestions to implement sooner rather than later.

I also need to emphasize that many of these suggestions require practice and patience. Be patient with yourself and with others. Change is difficult, but as long as you're committed to the goal and heading in the right direction, you'll see improvement, even if it is slow. Baby steps still bring movement.

Last, it is important to highlight a recent conversation I had with a student regarding the suggestions in the book. During this section of the class, she wrote me an email exclaiming that her team was doing many of the things listed in these suggestions, *but her team was still terrible!* This brings up a very important point. These suggestions are intended to be applied with caring and heartfelt intent to improve the workplace. Superficial attempts to "check the box" by applying these principles will be quickly noticed by team members. Also, sometimes trust needs to be developed first before drastic changes are made. Remember the story

DOI: 10.4324/9781003269038-19

from Chapter 8, the team traveling up the mountain? After being burned so many times by leaders, team members can become jaded, untrusting of a new (or old) leader's performance. This was the case in my student's organization. The team was untrusting of their "box-checking" manager and therefore unwilling to commit to the goal (focus) and the plan (direction) that the manager outlined for future success despite the manager's half-hearted attempts to improve teamwork.

Depending on the situation of your team, please remember, as previously stated, that these things take time. Sometimes it requires change to be made heart by heart, mind by mind, person by person. Stick to it though. A unified team is worth it. As I said in the introduction, I'm a realist, not a "rainbows and butterflies" optimist. This stuff works. We just need to use the right lures (Fishing Ninja) to get results.

In this section, we dive into specific practices, or potential lures, for each of the four components of unity: focus, direction, trust and conflict. As you read through the suggestions, take notes on can be applied in your team to increase unity. Maybe some of these ideas will spark other ideas that may improve unity. I look forward to hearing your success.

The first suggestion applies to all four unity components and is near and dear to everyone's heart, meetings.

Chapter 12

How to Hold Effective Meetings

The first application point to increase team unity affects all four components, and it addresses one of the most despised workplace requirements of all time: meetings. I have no doubt that just in reading the word "meetings," negative thoughts were stirred. Some may have even laughed out loud. Maybe some gave nose exhales. We all have special feelings about meetings, but I thought this was an excellent place to start because what better time is there to increase unity than when we have everyone together?

I am not anti-meeting. Rather, I'm anti–useless meetings. Many meetings are useless. There are several reasons for this, but the reason why I start this chapter by addressing meetings is because meetings can be a positive, uplifting and even enjoyable experience. They can even be unifying. Not every time. Not every meeting. But there's tremendous room for improvement for our usage of meetings.

A meeting is a gathering—virtual or in person—of people to discuss a topic or topics. They can be formal or informal. They can be for any amount of time. The meetings most people complain about are the formal, stuffy meetings where many people are gathered in a room. One person talks. The rest (pretend to) listen. Half the people in the room probably don't need to be there. An email would probably suffice in many cases. After the meeting, everyone goes about their day with very little reflection on the information shared in the meeting. When I mention the need for improving meetings when training or consulting, I often hear, "Oh, I thought we were the only ones with a problem with meetings." If you despise meetings, you're not alone . . . definitely not alone.

People find meetings frustrating for a variety of reasons. Frustrated team members are not happy team members, which means they're less unified, less interested in goal or direction, perform less, etc. There are several scholarly articles on the subject and many books for increasing meeting effectiveness[1,2] Given that meetings are excellent tools (when used correctly) for increasing focus, direction and trust and reducing conflict, I wanted to make sure to at least mention some good habits for increasing

DOI: 10.4324/9781003269038-20

meeting effectiveness. Fortunately, the most suggested improvements for formal meetings are actually some of the easiest to implement.

In summary, meetings need to be

- Efficient
- Effective

and

- Enjoyable

I call these the three Es of meetings (maybe I should coin the word Meeetings, meetings with three Es?). Here are some practices to achieve the three Es of meetings.

Meeting Practice #1 (Efficient): Respect Time

Time is a crucial resource. In a recent report by meeting scheduling service Doodle,[3] 37% of employees say unnecessary meetings are one of the biggest expenses in the company. Might seem like a bit of an exaggeration, right? Two-thirds of all meetings are deemed to be unnecessary, and 44% of the thousands surveyed stated that unnecessary meetings costs them so much time they were unable to finish their work on time. Meetings that waste time are a waste of (meeting) space.

Quick caveat: Some may take my focus on meeting efficiency as meaning that joking around is not allowed and that everything must be serious. That is definitely not what I'm saying nor is it my personality. Ninety-five percent of those surveyed say meetings can be a great time to build relationships. Allowing for humorous quips or brief sidetracks can be beneficial to the overall meeting effectiveness. The primary goal is likely to progress the project, but the secondary goal should be to build unity.

We are all a part of many groups and teams, each demanding a slice of our time. Respect the time of your team members. Start meetings on time. Don't have 100% attendance yet? If possible, start the meeting anyway. Respect the time of those who did make it a point to show up on time. Others will get the point and show up on time more in the future.

End the meeting on time. Most of the time work does not stop for a meeting. It continues to pile up. Telling your boss you're late with your project because you were in meetings probably won't suffice. There are a million things to do, but a person must pause everything they are doing in order to attend a meeting. Some even have activities planned immediately after the meeting. Extending the current meeting could upset a person's schedule for the rest of the day. End the meeting on time so team members can go back to being productive employees. If you need to extend the meeting, ask permission.

Many meetings become vastly less effective once the time has expired anyway. If there are still topics to be discussed, ask who is available to stay beyond the time; then see what you can do with the remaining crew. Many things discussed in a meeting with everyone present actually only apply to a few people or can be discussed after the meeting in a post-meeting meeting. Those having post-meeting meetings can then share the results of their discussion after the meeting. Using post-meetings helps meetings to stay on topic, end on time and increase efficiency and effectiveness because the key people can discuss on their own time as long as they would like and then report back to the group.

Meeting Practice #2 (Effective): Make Sure Stuff Gets Done

As a young employee, I remember one director stating in a meeting, "There's over $1,000,000 worth of salaries in here, and no one has an answer?" Think about the cost of the meeting. If you were to add up all the wages of the people in the meeting, is it worth $X to have that meeting? If it is, great, make sure that the items you identify in the meeting actually get done, or you're wasting how much the organization just paid for that meeting.

Many committees exist in organizations that seem to only exist to meet like that's the sole purpose of the committee. After a presentation to a group of regional business leaders, I was asked, "How do you know when it's time to disband a committee or board?"

My response was, "Well, if you're asking this question, then now is probably the time."

My response was received with laughter and a room full of nodding heads. We then discussed the issue. The committee did nothing. For more than a year, they had zero results to show. The company was continuing to provide resources for these people to meet regularly, but the group hadn't provided a single identifiable result in several *months*. We discussed the group at length and came up with a solution, but for business leaders who thrive on success, seeing a group accomplish nothing was so frustrating that it had been the topic of several executive meetings for months. I made sure to point out the irony that the executive group—which *hadn't done anything for months* to fix the situation—was complaining about a group that *hadn't done anything for months*. Again, the response was met with laughter and nodding heads. There were over 40 businesses represented in the room, and all of them understood exactly what I was talking about. It happens everywhere.

Not accomplishing anything is one of my biggest meeting complaints of all time. Efficiency and effectiveness are extremely important to me. Talking all day long and not resolving anything is extremely frustrating.

Sometimes a good brainstorming session is great, but when every meeting seems to be talking and reporting with no plan for improvement or action, that's a big problem.

To build a better reputation for your meetings, they must be worth something. They must actually make a difference. They must be seen as an investment instead of a cost. To do all this, they must accomplish something—get stuff done, move things forward. This starts with preparedness and ends with follow-up.

Meeting Practice #3 (Effective and Efficient): Be Prepared—With an Agenda

Being prepared for a meeting is essential for the facilitator as well as the attendee. The facilitator needs to know what the goal of the meeting is and what is going to be discussed. And an agenda needs to be provided to team members at least a day in advance.

Suggesting agendas is often met with a lot of resistance. I often hear, "Yeah, but I already know what I'm going to talk about." I have no doubt that meeting facilitators know what they're going to talk about, but no one else does.

Share with your team what you'd like to discuss, so they also can come prepared—especially if you hope to find a resolution to a problem. Give people time to think. Meetings will be far more effective if team members know what they will need to talk about. In fact, I could write an entire book called *The Power of Ponder*. Okay, maybe I won't call it that, but there is great power in pondering a topic or situation. Just thinking about a topic throughout the day can cause ideas to form so that when it's time for the meeting, team members show up with ideas to share. In fact, inspiration most often comes from pondering!

Providing an agenda at least a day before the meeting provides opportunities for the members to ponder the topics and participate in the meeting. Not everyone will take advantage of the time to ponder, but many will. Agendas provided before the meetings increase engagement.

Agendas do not to be extremely detailed, page-long point-by-point agendas. Maybe the big meetings would benefit from such an agenda, but often for the less formal meetings, a simple "Hey, we're going to be working on ideas to benefit the children, so come with at least three of your own ideas." or "Hey, we've been really struggling to increase production, so after the reports we are going to spend the rest of the meeting coming up with ways to increase production. Be prepared to discuss." Both phrases are sure to at least get people thinking before the meeting.

Also, regarding agendas, one of the biggest issues facilitators face is getting off subject. There may be some excellent points that need to be discussed, but an agenda helps keep everyone in line. Think of it as a contract between the meeting facilitator and the team members. You're saying, "If you give me an hour of your time, we'll discuss these things and solve these issues at a minimum." Then, if someone gets off topic, you can point to your "contract" and say, "Hey, that is an excellent point, but we only have x amount of time left, and we have a few more issues to discuss." You can postpone the topic to next meeting or to a post-meeting meeting. (Big fan of the post-meeting meetings. Can you tell?)

Or maybe you discover that team member X brings up an excellent point that needs to be discussed first before the agenda items. Perfect. Let everyone know that you're changing the agenda to cover the new topic. Then, at the end of the meeting, you can set up a post-meeting meeting, schedule a follow-up meeting or ask for permission from meeting attendees to stay longer.

Meeting Practice #4 (Effective): End Every Meeting With a Review of Everyone's Action Items

You all can't see me right now, but I'm getting excited just writing about meetings. For people to stay committed to the goal and the plan, they need to know what the next steps are, and they need to be accountable for those next steps. Assign action items during the meeting and review the action items at the end of the meeting. Assign deadlines or follow-up dates of the action items. Review action items at the end of the meeting by calling people by name and stating what they have volunteered or been "voluntold" to do.

Perhaps the most important part of an action item list is that someone actually follows up with the action items to make sure they're getting done by the date agreed on in the meeting. If it cannot get done by that date, agree to a new date, but there needs to be a date and follow-up to those dates.

People need to report back after they accomplish an action item. Their task is not complete until they report back to the group. Reporting back to the group is motivational. Others see what is getting done. It reminds other group members that they need to accomplish their assignment, and it helps people to see that other people in the group are committed to getting stuff done, so they should probably step up and help out as well.

Meeting Practice #5 (Enjoyable): Plan Something Fun

Meetings should be enjoyable. This doesn't mean every part of every meeting has to be enjoyable, but there should be something to look forward to, especially if there's resistance to attending a meeting. Everyone is already pausing their day to attend the meeting. Might as well make it something that people might enjoy. Providing food is common, but it could be recognition, talking about group or company success, upcoming products, holiday party ideas, etc. I've heard many great ideas, but food is my favorite.

"*If you* build it *feed them, they will come.*" Food brings people together. For many decades of my life, I have been involved in Boy Scouts. We used a common phrase based on a famous quote from a 1989 Kevin Costner movie, *Field of Dreams*. In the movie, Ray Kinsella (Kevin Costner) is a struggling corn farmer in Iowa. One night, when walking through his cornfield, he hears a voice give him instruction in a cryptic phrase, which begins his journey of self-discovery. The cryptic phrase was so popular that nearly every person in America alive in the 1980s and 1990s has, at some point, quoted some version of the phrase "If you build it, he will come." Even Tony Hawk, the skateboarding champion and successful entrepreneur, quoted this movie before the Pacifico 2021 Vert competition.[4] They asked why he, at 53 years old, decided to participate in the event. His response," I mean, if you build it, he will come. . . . I'm a big supporter verts (the name of the event) so I wanted to show my support." In Boy Scouts, we often used the phrase, "If you feed them, they will come." It is amazing how much attendance increases when you advertise that lunch is provided. But there's more to providing food than just gaining attendance. Food brings people together.

Several years ago, I had just been promoted to supervisor at large manufacturing company in Fort Worth, Texas. I thought I was someone special, moving up the company quickly, getting a large increase in pay. I thought I was exactly what this area needed to turn around. What a learning experience that was! Every person on my union team had been at the company much longer than me—and had far more experience than me. A few of my people were twice my age, working on their second retirement. On top of that, it was a rough environment.

My team had the great ability to point out all of my flaws—and weren't shy about pointing them out to my face. Long story short: We became an outstanding team that had a tremendous impact on operations. There were many, many contributing factors to that success, but one of the key ones, I believe, was food.

Our weekly meetings had been physically attended but not necessarily mentally attended. It was tough at first finding common ground with everyone, but I did discover we certainly all had one thing in common: we all enjoyed eating. So, I used that to our advantage. I decided to establish a potluck.

The team loved the idea.

Surrounding leadership resisted it, stating that I would never be able to do anything with union employees because they resisted everything.

I didn't see that at all. I saw a group of 21 employees who all loved to eat, myself included, so why not?

We established ground rules. No one was forced to bring anything. It was 100% voluntary. I told everyone I was bringing in food and that they were welcome to bring in food as well if they wanted. The first potluck was a huge success! Most everyone brought in food. Bacon-wrapped jalapeños, hash browns, donuts, breakfast sandwiches, fruit, breakfast casserole, so much food! We loved it. We decided to continue it but to limit it to just four people per week.

For more than 52 consecutive weeks, we had an excellent breakfast for our Thursday team meeting, but the key wasn't the food. The key is what the food caused us to do. We ate together. When you gather to eat, you talk. When you talk, you get to know each other. You build social trust. Social trust is critical for higher performing teams, as we've discussed, because that's what gets ideas flowing. When ideas are flowing, it creates a community of creativity. Creativity often leads to innovation. Innovation often leads to extraordinary teams that outperform other teams.

That is exactly what happened to us. Gathering once a week to eat and talk was critical in helping us grow from a group of frustrated employees into a group of trusted colleagues that stayed in touch long after our team dispersed. Our required weekly meeting was our reason for gathering. But food gave us a reason to open up, to share.

I've seen many managers play games or have some sort of activity that allows for some positive interactions. This is great as well. Some of my earliest memories are going to work with my mom on a few occasions. My mom was an excellent radiology manager at a major children's hospital in Texas. I remember going to her meetings. Her employees raced to the meetings. They fought over chairs. They talked and joked on the way to the meetings, in the meetings, after the meetings. She was excellent at unifying teams. One of her tactics was playing games. Carnival games, matching, competitions, drawings, all sorts of fun activities. She still covered correctional items that needed to be discussed, but the meeting started and ended with positivity, and her employees appreciated it.

Meeting Practice #6 (Enjoyable): Use Meetings to Celebrate Success

Another critical component of meetings is to celebrate success. Did an employee do something great that deserves to be recognized? Did the team achieve something great? If so, point it out. Celebrate it!

Sometimes you might have to get creative, like the NBA. The NBA uses statistics to share key points about players and how outstanding accomplishments are, but there are actually a team of statisticians that are constantly seeking new things to celebrate or new reasons to cause excitement. Want to know what the record is for three-pointers made in the second half of an away playoff game by a bench player or want to know how many Tuesday games have been won by one team versus another? Listen to the announcers. Someone feeds them these interesting facts that they share with the audience with the intent of adding interest and excitement into the game, to make people go, "Really? How about that?!"

There is always something that can be celebrated. Maybe it's the first week the entire team showed up on time to the meeting, or maybe it's the first month no one has burned popcorn in the microwave or maybe it's the 15th consecutive week of someone not clicking "reply all" to mass emails. Whatever it is, discover it and share it along with the other stuff. People love it.

Now that we've explored meetings, we will dive into how to increase each component of team unity.

Notes

1. Rogelberg, S. G. (2019). *The surprising science of meetings: How you can lead your team to peak performance.* Oxford University Press.
2. Harvard Business Review Press. (2016). Hbr guide to making every meeting matter.
3. The State of Meetings 2019. (2019, May 2). Doodle Blog. Retrieved from https://en.blog.doodle.com/state-of-meetings-2019/
4. Games, X. (2021). Pacifico Skateboard Vert Best Trick: Full Competition | X Games 2021. YouTube. YouTube. Retrieved from www.youtube.com/watch?v=rfllxl5kfik

Chapter 13

Increasing Team Focus

Increasing focus is interesting because it's about more than just goal set-ting. It requires gaining commitment from the team members. These sug-gestions will help.

Identify a Competitor

"The enemy of my enemy is my friend." Sometimes to get people to com-mit to a goal, they need to have a common person, organization or team they are trying to outperform. It could even be that they are competing against their own scores. Whatever it is, getting the team to unify their focus on outperforming another competitor is an extremely powerful way to unify a team.

There are television shows built around competitions with many great examples of people unifying to overcoming a competitor. Many shows are quite famous such as *The Amazing Race, Survivor* or even *America's Got Talent*. I'm a huge fan of competitive reality TV. When I have a chance, I enjoy watching people work together to overcome obstacles, especially if I'm learning in the process. I stumbled across *The Rap Game*. It absolutely captivated my attention.

Rap is an art. It tends to get a negative reputation for the rough lyrics that are often used by artists to tell their story, but that's just it: Rap is a powerful way tell a meaningful story, to send a message. Those who are proficient at lyrics are referred to as artists, as they should be. Rap is definitely an art form that many attempt, but only few make it. Several singing shows exists to help identify the next pop artist, but rap wasn't provided such opportunities until Jermaine Dupri's *The Rap Game* was created to identify young artists that deserved a shot.

Jermaine Dupri is no novice in identifying talent. Not only is he an accomplished artist himself, but he has also produced, managed or col-laborated with such famed artists as Kriss Kross, Bow Wow, Da Brat, Mariah Carey, Monica, Pharrell Williams, Jay-Z and Usher. His favorite part about the music industry is growing talent and making music. He

DOI: 10.4324/9781003269038-21

decided to use his talents and contacts to create opportunities for five young rap artists. The winners receive a recording contract with Jermaine's label So So Def. His team chooses five artists to compete by watching their videos posted online. Those who are chosen fly to Atlanta with their managers and move into one of only five bedrooms. Each week they are presented with a challenge. The contract could launch any of the young kids to stardom. Managers compete. Kids compete. The competition gets fierce.

The show is mostly an individual competition, but every season Jermaine throws out a situation in which the competitors are forced to work together.

"Music is a team environment. You can't make it in the industry alone. You may feel that you're all competitors, but the reality is you all need each other to continue growing the art of rap."

Jermaine Dupri created a situation that unified a tremendously splintered group. It's an excellent example of how a common "enemy" (competition) can unify a group.

Season three started with friction. Tally, a person that was cut early in season two, was brought back and instantly entered a feud with Deetronada. By week six, the competition had increased from petty arguments to pointed lyrical jabs and claims at being number one. There were more civil moments, but the young rappers and their managers had several altercations over the previous five weeks. This would not be the most likely group to collaborate with each other until they were presented with a challenge.

During a radio interview with the Durtty Boyz from Atlanta's Hot 107.9, the Boyz issued a challenge to Jermaine. They had met the five rappers competing in season three a few weeks prior. This time, they claimed to find a rapper that was so good that he deserved to be on *The Rap Game* possibly more than some of the other contestants. They challenged Jermaine's group to a cipher, a circular jam session sometimes turned into informal rap battles. They claimed that their contender could beat all five of them, and if he did, that Jermaine would have to give him a spot on the show cutting one of the current contestants in order to give the new person a shot. After several seconds passed, and with thousands listening, Jermaine accepted the challenge. If the contender beat all five contestants, then one of the contestants would be sent home and replaced by the contender. Emotions were high.

After the radio interview, the managers were anxiously waiting to discuss the challenge with their young rappers. None of the contestants were thinking about how they were going to outperform each other or who was going to stand out at the end of the week. Instead, they were focused and committed to one goal: not allowing the contender to steal a spot in the house. Here's just a few of their comments:

What I'm gonna tell all five of y'all is that no matter how y'all feel about each other, y'all better get in there and do what the hell y'all gotta do and make sure nobody else come in here in this house.

—King Roscoe's manager

I'm willin' to fight for everyone else in this house because I'm already comfortable with them . . . having someone else leave and someone else move in just won't feel right. . . . We all have our issues, but we all fam at the end of the day.

—Nova

I would like everyone to come together as one because I feel like it's a statement. . . . I'll do everything in my power to help any of them.

—Ekko, Nova's manager

Ain't nobody comin' in this house, shut yo mouth. Hey! Ain't nobody comin' in this house, shut yo mouth. Hey.

—Deetronada

All competitive feelings among the group disappeared and instead were focused on a single competitor. Contestants were helping each other with lyrics, and managers were supporting other artists. The five contestants and five managers were a team to take down their rival. No one talked about who Jermaine was going to cut that week. No one tore each other down. They were focused and committed to overcoming the challenge of protecting their house.

It's true that the show is edited, and we saw what the producers wanted us to see. But at the end of the week as Jermaine was reviewing their performance, even he mentioned how there was a fire ignited in them that he hadn't seen before. They weren't afraid of going home. That threat was present every week as each rapper was eliminated. Now they were fighting to protect each other from an external threat. It was a unified group that used each other's energy to add to their own. They were connected in mind and heart.

Finding a common enemy can take several forms. I've seen a seventh-grade teacher tell his students that they had to stick together because "seventh grade was the best." Sounds funny to think about, but it was a belief he promoted frequently and saw the fruits of when they started sticking up for each other against harassment from eighth graders. When he asked his students about one particular altercation in the hallway, they happily exclaimed that other seventh graders could make fun of another seventh grader, but no eighth grader was allowed to. I don't promote making fun of each other, but even 12- and 13-year-olds understand that we are stronger together against a common foe.

On a bigger scale, we've recently seen common enemies in global warming, high school graduation rates, recycling, COVID-19, poverty, homelessness, special needs and so much more. Using the COVID-19 pandemic as the "enemy" that needed to be combatted by something good, John Krasinski, the actor known for such shows as *The Office, The Quiet Place* and *Jack Ryan* created a good news network called *Some Good News* or SGN. The response was huge, as people shared his videos of good things happening all over the world thousands of times with millions of views. Many other people started sharing their good news during the quarantine, as we focused and committed to showing the world that despite the constant negativity, there is good in the world.

Think about what "common enemy" all of your team members have to compete against. It could be outperforming the previous team or previous record, it could be another company or maybe it is a risk from an external competitor. A common enemy is an excellent way to help increase focus.

Talk the Talk

If you want to increase focus, direction or trust, you have to set the example. It helps if you show your team that the goal is very important in your life. Show them that this goal is so important to you that you talk passionately about it. Many leaders do talk about their goals but not near frequently enough.

You may have heard of commercial and residential real estate agents talking about the importance of location. Location is so important that it is often repeated three times. Location, location, location. For a brick-and-mortar retail store, it is extremely important. It has to be a place where the target audience sees it on a regular basis, where it is convenient for people to stop buy. It's well-lit and safe. It has complementary stores surrounding it. A good location will help your store be successful.

Well, in the same vein, every team leader should communicate, communicate, communicate.

Communicating is more than just talking about a goal. Make sure your message is being seen frequently and in a variety of ways. Others in your organization need to see that this message or goal is at the forefront of your mind, just as it should be for them. They need to see that it isn't just a fleeting thought but that you're serious, so they should be, too. You bring it up in meetings. You ask them questions about it. The message is discussed in informal meetings. Make posters. Make signs. Show charts. Use graphs. Give prizes. Recognize effort. In informal meetings. Formal meetings. Talk about the goal.

One company I work with created a reward for safety, in which the leadership team would wash the cars of their employees if they met their safety goal. When they did, the company celebrated with T-shirts and set up a car washing line staffed by management. They showed they cared about the goal so much that they were willing to stop work for a day and wash cars.

That's a powerful message, but that's not the only message they sent. They wrote memos, put up flyers, used formal meetings, rewarded safe behavior, had a day counter since their last accident, celebrated good decisions and hired a reputable training group to train on safety. Everyone in the plant knew this company valued safety.

If you're committed to this goal, make sure you're communicating your commitment to this goal via both verbal and nonverbal communications.

Walk the Walk

Your actions have to show that you're totally committed to the team's goal. Similar to "talk the talk," your actions send nonverbal communications to the rest of the team about what you value. Imagine how it would look if you were requiring mandatory overtime and pushing for double output while coming in late and leaving early every day. I get it. Employees should worry about their own affairs and not yours. That is true . . . however, by shirking the same behaviors you expect of them, you are telling them that this goal is so important that everyone needs to make sacrifices, except you. That doesn't sit well with followers.

Earlier in the book, I shared a story about Lord Shackleton and how he held his team together to survive 15 months in Antarctica.[1] It goes without saying that the task wasn't easy. For the first three months in Antarctica, they were trapped. The ice shelves had pinched their ship. They could not escape, so they rode with the ice shelves.

Life wasn't too bad at this point. They had all the comforts of their ship, plus a large number of rations and other supplies to help keep them warm and fed. They were dry, and the ship helped protect them from the frigid wind and precipitation. As the ice shelves squeezed the ship tighter, the boards began to bow and break under the pressure. The first plank to snap startled the men because the sound was like a revolver being discharged at close range. It was a sound they never got used to. Eventually, they had to abandon ship.

Abandoning the ship was an extremely difficult decision for Lord Shackleton to make because he knew that their chances for survival were drastically reduced without it.

It troubled Shackleton to ask so much of his men. He had survived in harsh conditions before, but many of them had not. What started off as an exciting journey had now turned into a fight for survival. He gathered his men together and shared a short speech, in which he explained that nothing but the bare necessities would be allowed to continue on the journey. He gave them their list of items they each were allowed to carry: the clothes on their backs, two pairs of mittens, six pairs of socks, two pairs of boots, a sleeping bag and two pounds of personal possessions. "No article has any value when measured against our survival. . . . Everything is replaceable except your lives."

At this point, Shackleton set the example. He took out his Bible, a beautiful book given to him by Queen Alexandra just the year before. He tore out two pages and placed the book in the snow. He then took out his gold watch, a gold cigarette case and several gold coins and placed them in the snow as well. He then turned and walked away. Lord Shackleton had set the tone of what was expected. His men understood to what extent they should do the same. They followed. He wasn't asking them to do something he wasn't willing to do himself. He walked the walk.

It is extremely powerful to see a leader, someone who one might consider "above" a task, doing that lowly task. Disney has something called the "Disney Swoop." When a Disney employee is walking, regardless of their station, level, etc. if a Disney employee sees trash on the ground, the employee is encouraged to continue walking but to swoop down and scoop up the trash, depositing it in the nearest (and strategically placed) trash receptacle. It isn't the most fun task to do, but Disney is about delivering an experience that is difficult to do with litter.

Trash is a negative experience. People are paying a lot of money at Disney World to leave negativity behind; thus, it is every employee's job to help with trash by employing the Disney Swoop. It just so happens one employee saw Lee Cockerell—executive vice president of Disney, previous vice president of several other companies, best-selling author and all-around good guy to have around—perform the Disney Swoop while on his way to a meeting.

> I was walking with Lee to his next meeting. He had a large entourage as someone at his level normally did. They were discussing some pretty serious topic when Lee spots an ice cream wrapper on the ground. Without missing a beat, he swoops down and picks it up and places it in the trash. He continues walking and talking without missing a beat! I saw that and thought "Man, if Lee Cockerell can do the swoop, then what excuse do I have to not do the swoop?!"[2]

The employee informed me that since that time, he has read all four of Lee's books and decided to make a career change because of it. That's some serious swooping impact! It's great to talk about a goal, but when you can show that you are also committed to this goal with both verbal and nonverbal communication, it is extremely motivating.

Goals Need Reminders

A common occurrence among most of the stories in this chapter about focus is that they almost all include some sort of reminders. Reminders can be anything that help remind employees about the goal. They should be simple. Putting 54 reminders about 54 different goals will make it difficult for employees to remember and follow, no matter how many reminders you institute.

Disney Dreams

I'm a huge fan of theme parks, as you may have guessed from reading my examples in this book. To me, they're the perfect business. Theme parks are intricate businesses that are so much more than just rides, and the detail is incredible. They might have water treatment plants, jails, urgent clinics, mechanics, engineers, designers, decorators, chefs and SCUBA divers, and the list could go on and on. The complexity of a theme park is outstanding, and all of this complexity is for a single purpose: to deliver an opportunity to escape.

While providing escapism is a noble cause, the people providing this escape experience are normal, working people. While we're walking around with sweet treats, they're in the hot sun, sweeping up trash and wearing uncomfortable uniforms. They're people with responsibilities, relationships, career stresses and family issues just like you and me, yet they're asked to set it all aside for the benefit of the guest.

To keep their cheery disposition, they need reminders.

If you had to create a list of reminders for employees at this level, you might think of items like the following. Remember to

- Tie your shoes.
- Tuck in your shirt.
- Have no stains on your clothes.
- Smile.
- Consider the customer is there to escape negativity; don't add to it.
- Realize this is your hundredth time hearing this problem, but it's only their first time to have this problem.
- Check trashes regularly.
- Check condiments.
- Focus on safety, safety, safety.

The list could be endless, depending on where you are in the park and what role you are playing. You might post this extremely long list, or you might use Disney's approach to reminding their employees about the roles they play in customer escapism.

Before any employee goes into the guest area of the park where the guests are—Disney calls it "on stage"—they walk past a mirror. The mirror is a physical reminder to be in character because the employee is part of a show. Other than being a mirror for cast members to check their teeth, hair and makeup before going on stage (they're not *that* high quality), there are several positive consequences to this practice. I'd like to highlight two.

1.   It reminds employees of the *temporal nature* of their role. Off stage, they're allowed to be who they would like to be. All Disney is asking is that when they are onstage, that they be the character they were hired to be. This reminds them: *You are not John or Sally. You are the Churro vendor (Disneyland), John or Sally from Detroit.* There is a lot of power for employees in accepting their roles and realizing they are only roles. If someone doesn't like their role, they can hang up their costume and walk away at the end of the day. But essentially, the request is made: "For your shift, please be the character you were hired to be."
2.   The mirror is a physical reminder that the guests are expecting to be in a show in which they are the stars. While at Disney, guests have opportunities to participate in their own child-like fantasies. They can soar around the world, join Aerosmith in their tour limo, help the seven dwarves with their mine train or fly on the back of a Banshee. Guests are there to experience escapism. It is up to the cast members to provide that for guests. The mirror is a simple, cost-effective, physical reminder of their role in creating an experience for their guests.

I have no doubt that after several months, the effect of walking past the mirrors wears off. In fact, by the time this book is published, I wouldn't be surprised to hear that Disney ditched the mirrors. No problem. Reminders should be refreshed because eventually they become part of our daily landscape, blending in instead of standing out. Reminders need to continue catching our attention like Department of Transportation road signs.

Engaging Road Signs

I've driven in over 40 states in the United States, and there are some creative signs used by the Department of Transportation (DOT) to remind drivers to be safe. The best part is that they change just about every week.
Arizona's DOT has some great ones. Here are a few:

•   "Drinking and driving go together like peas and guac."
•   "Cut off? Don't get bad blood. Shake it off." (referencing Taylor Swift's song lyrics)

- "Aggressive driving is the path to the dark side." (referencing the *Star Wars* movie franchise)

Because they change, you always want to read them. Because you read them, you're always reminded.

Make your reminders interesting and change them up regularly. Other reminders could be banners, emails, lunches, T-shirts, messages in meetings—and many more physical, conversational and even digital.

Spread Appreciation

During one visit to Disney World's Magic Kingdom, I was fortunate to visit their employee building. The theme park that is enjoyed by more than 20,000,000 people a year is iconic in its look and appearance. The employee stations where lockers and costumes are kept for nearly 70,000 employees is not iconic in appearance. It looks and feels similar to many employee buildings I've visited throughout the years, but this was Disney, so of course there were a few Disney touches.

Every year, thousands of visitors send thank you cards, notes and letters to the staff at Disney World to let the employees know how appreciated their efforts are in assisting guests with escaping the troubles of the real world. These letters are read, and many are kept and used as reminders to employees that what they do matter. Within a short distance of entering the employee building, I passed a wall dedicated to notes to Disney World employees from customers. There were a couple of employees reading the notes before heading off to their shifts. I couldn't help but stop and take a look. Many of the letters talked about family struggles or hard times that were difficult to overcome but said that because of outstanding employees, they were able to let go just for a short while and enjoy life. Many highlighted specific employee actions. On the opposite wall was a video of different people and families thanking the Disney staff for providing excellent service during their vacations. It was an excellent reminder to keep employees focused on performing their roles well because doing so mattered.

On that note, appreciation goes a long way to remind people that what they're doing matters. If you see someone doing something great, thank them. It's more powerful if you thank them for their specific actions. A simple, "Hey, I saw you pick up that trash as you walked by it. Thank you for doing that. That was great to see." As a leader, you'll be far more likely to see those good actions repeated than if you just say a simple thank you.

Appreciation in the Classroom

I started off as a seventh-grade history and English teacher. I loved teaching seventh grade. I knew it wasn't my forever career, but the two years I did it were an excellent time for me.

Of course, there were hard times during that period, too. Sometimes they were self-inflicted. Sometimes they were because of the students. Other times they were because of administration.

During my first year of teaching, I found that my classroom management skills could use a little help. I was having a great time with the students, but this school was in a low socio-economic area. Many of my students had experienced a variety of abuse. Many had behavioral issues. It was rough.

The ideal situation is when the teacher, the parents and the student combine to create a unified team to grow the mind of the child. Many of these parents were working multiple jobs and struggling to pay rent. Unfortunately, this left little time to spend with their children. Many of the students had issues with behavior, causing parents to be inundated with phone calls from the school. Parents would often respond to a call from the school with an exasperated "What did my child do now???" It was not fun to call parents, but it was something that unfortunately happened quite often.

One day during a meeting, the administration suggested that we call parents at least once every nine weeks for *good* reasons. That is, they suggested we call to thank and tell the parents something good about the child—and nothing else. No negativity in that phone call at all. Just a good phone call. If we had something negative to say, then we had to make the negative call another day.

I enjoyed being with my students, but this was a rough assignment. There were many students who were in fights, drugs, stealing, dealing and all sorts of crazy things that 12- and 13-year-old kids should not have to be a part of. The kids were struggling. The parents were struggling. The teachers were struggling, and we were told to find a reason to be grateful.

I made my first phone call. I decided to call an easy one. It was to the parents of a student who made straight As. I don't think these parents had ever received any phone calls about their child. This is about how the phone call went:

ME: Hello, Mrs. _____, I was calling about your daughter, _____.
PARENT: Oh my! Is everything alright? What happened?!
ME: No, no. Everything is fine. Actually, I was just calling to say that your daughter is consistently on time with her assignments and has excellent comments during class. I really appreciate her.
PARENT: Thank you. That was nice of you. Is there anything else?
ME: Nope. Just wanted to let you know that.

PARENT: Wow. Thank you. Well, you have an excellent day.
ME: Thank you. You, too!

Excellent phone call. The mom, despite having an excellent child, was genuinely surprised when the teacher called and said something good about her. It felt good. I tried a few more of my A students. Similar results. Some even led to some great conversations about their child—and about the parents.

I was having fun with this, but I was running out of A students.

Next, I chose one of my students who had behavioral problems. I seriously had to think about what to say about this student. He had turned in assignments late. He definitely was not an A student. He actually had to be prevented from fighting just that week. He didn't comment during class, but he was nice to his peers most of the time.

Then it hit me. This student had arrived on time every day last week! Sounds normal, but for him it was a big deal! I was going to go with that. Here's how that phone call went:

ME: Hello, can I speak to Ms. _____.
STUDENT: Umm, okay. May I ask who is calling?
ME: Yes. Hey there. This is Mr. Ross. How are you _____?
STUDENT: Umm, okay. Let me go get her.

(In the background, I hear him tell his mom that I was on the phone. Her response was not pleasant and was followed by:)

ME: Hello, Ms. _____. This is John Ross from the school. Your son's teacher for history and English.
PARENT: Oh hell! What did he do now?
ME: Oh, nothing. I'm actually calling for a good reason.
PARENT: Really? Why is that?
ME: Oh, your son showed up to class on time every day this past week. He was close a couple of times, but he made it. I know that was hard for him, but he made it. Just thought you should know that.
PARENT: (stunned) That's really why you called?
ME: Yes. Just wanted to let you know that he is trying in school.
PARENT: Wow . . . thank you. Thank you for the call.
ME: You're very welcome. Have a nice night.
PARENT: You, too! Thank you.

The call went well. In fact, it went very well. The next day, students raced into the classroom, exclaiming, "My mom was so happy! I thought I was in trouble when I heard you called, but that was awesome!" Many other comments about how happy their parents were echoed from half my students, accompanied by, "When are you going to call my parents?!" from the other half. They also received phone calls, of course.

The students loved that I did this. The parents loved it. I loved it. I saw an immediate result. I called the parents of half of my students that first night. I told parents I appreciated their child's effort, humor, punctuality, dedication, positive attitude, leadership, imagination and creativity. The next day, I saw more humor, more dedication, more positive attitudes, more leadership, more imagination and more effort. When I called the other half of the students, I received similar results.

My students shifted to trying to do good things and encouraging me to call their parents about it. When one student received a great grade on one of his tests, he exclaimed, "You should call my dad about this."

I replied, "You have your test. You go show him your test score." His dad was thrilled.

The results were not just from the students but also from the parents. This was a demographic of parents that don't typically volunteer at schools. After my phone calls, these parents were my biggest supporters. Any time I needed anything, literally anything (once I joked I needed lunch. I had it within minutes) they made sure I had more than enough. The results were tremendous! We had a great year.

It is true that there were many more factors into our successful year. It could be said that it was actually me who changed because I began noticing how great my students were. But I'd like to think that the parents, students and I *all* changed. We all were reminded that "we're in this together."

Expressing appreciation was definitely one of the changing points that year, reminding them that good behaviors did matter. Make sure to express specific appreciation to those around you even if it's difficult.

Apply the 25% Rule

During my research with a variety of groups, I noticed an interesting phenomenon: There were times when extremely motivated people (high in focus) with a history of success tended not to perform as well when put in a group with people who didn't seem to care much about the team's results (low in focus). I found this really interesting. I witnessed people who I knew were extremely interested in high achievement, but they seemed to show very little effort in some of their teams. I decided to investigate further.

It seems that a team will stoop to lower levels of commitment when at least 25% of the team is unmotivated or uncommitted to the goals. There are exceptions to this rule, such as the value of the reward being offered, but it seems that motivated, focused people feel that convincing one-quarter of the team to wake up and get on board is perceived to be too difficult, so they don't try.

Think about this for a second. In a team of four, having just one uncommitted member of the team that is low in focus is difficult to deal with. It's enough of a margin that you really can't just ignore them without being obvious. Trying to plan meetings knowing that one of the members is against the idea is rough. This will often lead to an unbalanced workload, with the motivated people doing most of the work, *allowing* the one uncommitted person to be a social loafer. Think about that statement. Sometimes, instead of addressing the lack of commitment, we ignore it and move on without them. This actually *allows* them to be a social loafer. They'll receive credit for being on the team, without having to do much of the work!

The psychology of the social loafer sounds like an excellent idea for my next book. Needless to say, though, when you have someone that is low in focus on your team causing imbalanced workloads, it often leads to relational conflict. This is a problem, and the problem seems to start when just 25% of the team is low on the focus scale.

So, what happens fewer than 25% of the team low in focus? Those low in focus tend to conform deciding to increase their commitment to the goal (increase focus) rather than disrupt the rest of the team. They may not give it their all, but they tend to at least go with the flow. Conformity is not a good scenario for reaching extraordinary levels of unity. Conformity produces a quiet team but not necessarily a unified team.

The point of introducing the 25% rule is to highlight how critical it is to make sure to work with the dissenters even though it is tempting to ignore them. Find out what is holding them up and why they seem to be against the goal. Get them on board. Once the dissension is below 25%, then comes the difficult task of finding the others that are just conforming and working with them. As famous football coach Pete Carroll of the NCAA football dominating University of Southern California Trojans in the 2000s and the tremendous turnaround story of the Seattle Seahawks in the 2010s says, "Each person holds so much power within themselves that needs to be let out. Sometimes they just need a little nudge, a little direction, a little support, a little coaching, and the greatest things can happen."

To create an extraordinary team, you need everyone to be extraordinary. Invest the time and energy into each person as an individual. In general, when most of the team "gets it" and only a few are resisting, start with the biggest dissenters, then work your way through the conformers until everyone is united in one heart and one mind. There are situations when some may have insurmountable reasons why they are not committing to a goal or a plan. Often it is because of relational conflict (they don't like the leader or other people on the team or feel slighted in some way), but there are many reasons that may exist. There are entire books written on this subject but remember to meet that person (those people) where they are at and work with them to build unity. Forcing unity is often not a good idea. It needs to be built.

Notes

1. Lansing, A. (2015). *Endurance: Shackleton's incredible voyage*. Basic Books.
2. Ross, J. (2019, December). If Lee Can Do it, So Can I! The Disney Swoop. personal.

Chapter 14

Increasing Team Direction

Improving direction is complicated. Getting people to understand and commit to a course of action seems simple, but it could require extended investment in employee development. No matter what though, it is definitely worth it. This chapter includes some practices that can help instill a sense of direction.

Create Lists

I know this is very basic, but do people in your organization know what they're supposed to do? In a study of 2.2 million employees at over 550 organizations, Gallup found that only about half of employees felt confident they know what their expectations are.[1] Think about your organization. What if half weren't able to truly commit to their roles because they weren't exactly sure what their roles were? Half of the employees are doing what they *think* is right but aren't able to commit with the full gusto of *knowing* what to do.

I always recommend lists first for the same reason information technology help desks always ask you to restart your computer. Sometimes we overlook the simplest fixes because we feel absolutely sure the issue is much deeper. Sometimes it isn't. Lists are extremely important. Even though we may have been told 100 times, sometimes we forget. Working is not our life (hopefully, anyway). Sometimes we all need a clear reminder of what we're supposed to do.

When possible, try providing a list, an actual written list, of expectations to be successful. Let them know what you expect them to do before the end of the day, end of the week or end of the month. Many people I've worked with have actually said they enjoy checklists because they actually enjoy checking things off the list. It's reassuring to know that you're making progress and doing what you're supposed to be doing.

Another benefit of lists is it allows new employees to hit the ground running. Remember what it felt like to be new? You were most likely disoriented, unsure of your work and trying desperately to remember

DOI: 10.4324/9781003269038-22

everyone's names. Trying to remember what your daily tasks are can bit overwhelming. Providing a simple list is nice because it reassures new employees about the expectations and gives them a language to use when talking to other people in the organization. Now they can go to their coworkers and ask specific task-related questions. This starts a good conversation among colleagues.

The downside to checklists is that employees may take the list as gospel truth and believe that if they accomplish everything on the list, then they must be doing awesome. We both know rarely does a list entail everything that needs to be done. Employees sticking strictly to the list might look like they are not fully focused—like they're just trying to get out of doing extra work. This isn't exactly fair for the employees. They were provided a list, and they accomplished the list. If you wanted them to do more, then why didn't you put more on the list? If lists are too long, then they become demoralizing because it appears as if the employee is being set up for failure. This makes the list a lot less effective. So, what is the correct solution? You cannot possibly write every little thing that you expect them to do. Here are a couple of suggestions:

- **Keep the list broad.** A broad checklist is good for employees who are dedicated and knowledgeable enough to be provided freedom. Keeping the list broad allows you to avoid writing tiny details. This requires more training from the leader. If an employee needs to provide report X every Tuesday, then make that a checkpoint. You don't have to write every detail required to create the report. Just make the report a bullet point on the list; then allow the employee the freedom (if possible) to accomplish report X, however they'd like as long as they do report X.
- **Provide multiple lists.** I use this concept for movie theaters. I've worked with many theaters across the country. I hear from managers that they're tired of their employees not doing all of their tasks correctly. Well, yeah, because everyone has a different standard for cleaning or preparing food. There needs to be a standard way of doing things, so that it is done the same way by any shift, any crew. The first thing I do is ask for the checklist. Normally, I find the checklist with stuff piled on top of it. When it's shown to me, I commonly hear, "Oh, no one looks at that." Frequently, it's outdated. An updated list, clearly posted, with leadership follow-up goes a long way. If your checklist is the standard, then that standard needs to be rewarded or enforced.
- **First article inspection.** There's a term in supply chain in which the first article of a new supplier is inspected to make sure the quality is as expected. Once that passes, the future inspections are spread out on a regular basis. Use this for checklists. Provide a list. Explain the list.

Show them what a good job looks like; then inspect their "first delivery" with a high level of scrutiny to ensure proper "delivery" of the job. Once they get the hang of it, you'll be able to check in every once in a while, but don't leave them alone until they know what a good job looks like and what the expectation of their delivery to you is.

Lists are excellent ways to help establish direction because they detail what to do and when to do it. Lists should be accompanied with the "why," and plenty of resources should be provided for the "how."

Implement Process Improvement

Sometimes it is our poor processes that get in the way of full commitment to the direction because it is frustrating to be a part of a process that is broken. I'm a huge fan of process improvement. I've been fortunate to lead several very successful projects and be a part of several more. If something is not being accomplished or if something is being done poorly, it could be because there is a poor process in place.

Several years ago, I interviewed an employee who had recently been trained in Lean/Six Sigma. Lean is the craft of removing unnecessary and often wasteful steps from a process. Six Sigma refers to the training on how to reduce errors with the target being six sigma, or 3.4 defects per million opportunities. The two are excellent when taught together because any process can be nearly without defect if enough steps are added, but then the process could take an hour just to pour a bowl of cereal. Sure, no milk would spill, but it took an hour! The role of Lean is to limit the amount of steps to increase efficiency.

Quick example: If you wanted to be sure that all the lights were turned off when leaving the house, you could make each member of your family walk through the house independently and check every room in the house. I have six people in my family. That would be six people doing a check on the whole house. Might be overkill, and it may take us 20 minutes to leave the house each time, but that would ensure no light would be left on. I have no doubt we would reach Six Sigma. However, that's a lot of unnecessary steps. Maybe just one person checks, or maybe on our way out the door everyone just turns out the lights as they walk to the door. That would be much faster and would probably yield similar results as the six independent checks in the original plan.

Lean and Six Sigma balance each other to provide necessary steps to reduce errors while reducing unnecessary steps. This makes the process more efficient and effective by removing waste such as excess inventory, movement, over-processing, over-production, waiting, transport and defects.

A supplier manager I interviewed was really enjoying his training in Lean/Six Sigma.[2]

"As I sat listening, all I could think was that I wasn't learning just another skill. I was learning a way of life. It is how I see everything. I even started looking at how I drive to work and how I go through a grocery store."

After one intensive week, he went back to his workstation with a renewed outlook on work but was disappointed upon noticing the inefficiencies of his own work department.

> Our job was to be the go-between for the project managers and the suppliers, making sure that everything arrived on time and at price or better. If anything was wrong with the supplier, we'd go out there to see what we could do to help. The problem wasn't suppliers. Almost all of our suppliers were excellent because we were a large company, and they wanted to keep our business. The biggest issue was with the project managers.

The team was given a seven-item checklist from their managers in order of importance. They were told that all seven items were important, but the supplier managers were to work on the first item first, then the second, etc. They were also told that project managers were the first priority. They were not on the list, but the supplier managers were required to drop everything they were doing to help the project managers they were supporting any time they called, emailed, texted, etc. You can probably see where this is going.

This employee had been at the company for several months and only just then realized that only the first and second items were being completed. Items three through seven were hardly touched. He asked around and discovered that no one on his team or other teams were able to even consider five through seven. The senior managers were frustrated at the lack of accomplishment, but they just accepted that was how work was done. They couldn't shorten the list because everything on the list was important. In other words, every person in the department was a failure, except some failed less than others.

This is a common scenario in the workplace. The team had a goal and a strategy to meet that goal, but it is difficult to commit to a strategy that seems impossible. Every single day, the team "failed," but instead of doing anything about it, they accepted it as life and decided to redefine failure as "normal" and thus it was okay. In essence, they redefined the strategy on their own to meet their needs even though the company still expected them to meet their performance measures.

> It was the weirdest thing. We weren't even close to accomplishing the things on our list, and everyone was okay with that, even though our raises and performance reviews were dependent on our successful completion of all seven tasks on a regular basis. When I asked

around, everyone said it was because I was new and that I'd get used to it. But I didn't want to get used to it. I wanted to get it done.

As part of his Lean/Six Sigma training, he was tasked with finding a project on which he could save time and money by fixing a process. He was inspired by the constant failure of everyone in his department. After many weeks of talking it over and modeling new processes with his manager, project managers and the process improvement team, they found the solution: The issue was the project managers.

The project managers were stressed and constantly being asked for updates. For some, their entire project would be held up by one part, so they would call and get updates. If we only managed one project manager, that wouldn't be a problem, but we tended to manage dozens of project managers, sometimes over 100 at a time. Some days we would spend so much time on the phone with the project managers that we would barely be able to accomplish item number one.

The solution was to provide a status report every Tuesday and Friday. The supplier managers would post their reports to a website. If project managers needed to know the status, they were instructed to look at the site. The project leads had ways to communicate back via the site by marking parts that were high priority—or parts that were "notify upon receipt," so they could move forward with their next steps in their projects.

The results were outstanding. The project managers were interrupting the workflow of the supplier managers less often. Project managers had less reason to call because they were always only a few days away from an update. On top of this, they could check the status of their parts any time of the day. The supplier managers were happier as well. The employees were able to regularly accomplish tasks one through five and even reach tasks six and seven on occasion. The employees were happier. In fact, several months later, the employees were still experiencing much higher levels of success and were more energized at work because of it.

The effort by the employee and process improvement team saved an estimated $250,000 a year in time and additional work that was able to be accomplished. The senior leader was promoted to director shortly after the completion of the project, where she was a supporter of even more process improvement projects.

Hindrances can be tremendous demoralizers. By now you've read over 200 pages about the importance of unity and the role of direction in unifying a team, but when people are being asked to accomplish a task and they're unable to do it, it's incredibly disheartening.

Processes are a great place to look for improvements in efficiencies and effectiveness.

Waste is a common hindrance to success. Here's a list and brief explanation of the waste discussed in most every process improvement training.[3] Take a look at the list and see if there's a way to reduce the waste in your organization by reducing any of these components.

- **Inventory.** Inventory cost money and time. A surplus of inventory reduces cash flow because the cash is tied up in the inventory, plus it takes up space and could go bad or out of style.
- **Motion.** Any time a human or item needs to move, it takes time and increases the chance for error. Think about a report that needs seven signatures. The report starts with you and then goes to person B and waits. Then it's walked to person C, then waits, etc. This doesn't even count the distractions along the way. Reduce movement.
- **Overprocessing.** Are there steps in the process that do not provide value? Using the example with turning off the lights before leaving the house, is it really necessary for six people to all check each room in the house?
- **Overproduction.** Make what is needed, when it is needed. Think of Little Caesar's. Yes, they have Hot-N-Ready pizza, but they have data that show how many pizzas they need and when they're needed. They only make more pizzas if they know a large order is coming up, but otherwise, they stick to the plan. No more. No less.
- **Waiting.** Anytime there's waiting, it's wasted time. The number one reason people dislike theme parks? It's not the cost. The cost would be more worth it if there was no waiting! Turns out theme parks don't like customsers waiting much either. If they're stuck in a line, they're less likely to spend money. Thus, Disney has the Lighting Lane, and Universal has the Express Pass and both parks use the virtual queue system so customers can walk around while "waiting" in line. More fun for the customer and more money for the park! A good project manager will anticipate the wait and fill the time with another task, but sometimes it's unavoidable.
- **Transport.** This involves delivery of goods or services. Lawn companies are far more effective if they have multiple lawns in one area that they could easily walk to instead of mowing one lawn, loading the truck and driving to another lawn.
- **Defects.** A defect effects reputation, but it also causes repairs or loss of income for replacement. Reduce the defects to save time and money.

Hoshin Kanri

Similar to process improvement strategies, learning about Hoshin Kanri (HK) was another life changer for me. HK is the number one most requested topic expansion. I agree. This little blurb on HK is not enough to explain the power of HK. My next book will have an entire chapter dedicated to HK.

Hoshin Kanri is Japanese for "management by direction" or "management compass." Essentially, it is a robust strategic deployment initiative. It is accomplished throughout all levels of an organization. The executives set the company goals, the next level sets the regional strategy that supports the executive strategy, the next level sets the department strategy that supports the regional strategy, the next level sets the team strategy that supports the department strategy and so forth.

Hoshin Kanri focuses on five main focus areas. For production, it's frequently *quality, cost, safety, people* and *delivery.* With slight adjustments, these could fit almost any industry.

The process starts off with the decision makers in a room, ten people or fewer (the more people you have, the longer it takes). The facilitator normally starts with an evaluation of the current status with such questions as "What do we do well?" and "What don't we do well?" This elicits a lot of discussion, which is followed by a discussion of questions like "What do we value?" and "Where do we want to be in five years?" Lots more discussion and sticky notes are used.

By the end of this meeting, people are normally amped up for change. Over the next two weeks (-ish, could be more or less), these same people slowly and methodically craft the strategy, setting one to two goals per focus area.

The list doesn't just stop there. The team also sets metrics to measure goal accomplishment, one to three strategies to implement in order to accomplish the goal, metrics to measure the strategies, timing on how frequently they will review the metrics and assignment of someone to keep track of all the goals and strategies.

This process creates an extremely detailed plan that is absolutely worth the time and energy to create. But the real magic of the HK is that everyone is on board with the plan because they all helped make it, and they all hold each other accountable to it. If something is not working, they fix it, and they fix it together. In other words, HK is a tool to build and commit people to a plan. It is a tremendous tool for building unity.

The first time I heard about HK was in the workplace from some new guy who later became an extremely impactful mentor. I was a project lead at a major manufacturing company that makes airplanes. My job provided me opportunities to work all over the plant with a wide variety of different leadership styles. One area was widely known to be the trouble spot, forward fuselage. The forward fuselage is the part where the pilot sit. It also includes the nose cap, space for the navigational and communication equipment and forward landing gear.

Forward was in a tough spot. They had their build instructions but could not seem to complete all of their steps during the time the component was in their area. Because of this, their mechanics were sent to the other areas so they could finish their steps in the next area—which then slowed down the build of the next component. Not only that, but their area also frequently produced a high level of quality defects—which were caught before the aircraft build was finished, but it slowed down the production process. Forward was in a bind, which caused the rest of the factory to be in a bind.

Several managers rotated in and out of forward fuselage. Mechanics were traded in and out. Several practices were tried. Most managers believed that it was just going to take time to build the aircraft quicker and that the learning curve would eventually catch up to building the aircraft faster, but the dial was not moving as quickly as they thought it would. The problem was starting to get noticed by their customers. Something had to be done soon.

Right about this time, a new director was hired. He had a successful career at a car company and was looking for a new challenge. While he was on a tour of the production facility, he fell in love with the aircraft and the city. He told the vice president giving the tour that he would love a job there. Within a short amount of time, he had arrived.

His first month with the company was humbling.[4] He was an accomplished manufacturing professional and knew that there were differences between automobile and aircraft manufacturing, but he didn't realize the differences were as big as they were. He respected the work the mechanics did. He tried to learn as much as possible. He walked through every job and through every shift. When he saw something that interested him, he'd ask, "Hey, whatcha doin?" or "Why are you doing it that way?" Slowly, he learned about the job.

He also learned a lot about the people. What he learned most, however, was how much they lacked a clear direction: "They weren't working toward anything. They all wanted to be a great area. They wanted to finish their work and improve quality, but they didn't know how. Energy was low. No one wanted to work in forward. It was a rough environment."

He realized that they needed something to work toward, that they needed direction. They needed a solid plan that everyone could get behind—a plan that was easily understood and something they could commit to. They needed to bring all of their mechanics back to the station. In order to do this, he'd have to lead the group to achieve something they'd never done before.

He started by presenting a goal. They were finally going to finish the forward fuselage before sending it to the next area which meant they would have to increase output and decrease defects. He socialized it, talking about how great it would be if they could accomplish it. When they asked how, that's when he brought up HK. He told them that by creating a plan together, they would be able to make the impossible possible. His team was against it from the start.

> I knew my team would be resistant to change, but they weren't just resistant. They were against it. You know how every team has its leaders? You know, you have formal leaders, then you have the real leaders, the ones everyone looks to. You know what I mean? Well, over the next month, I had identified who my informal leaders were. I started with them.

After several weeks of convincing his most resistant supervisors to just try HK, they finally decided to give it a shot. For two weeks, the leadership team met and discussed. There was plenty of task conflict, plenty of opinions, but in the end, the plan was made, the metrics were set. Now came the hard part.

> The hardest part of Hoshin Kanri is that first month when people aren't exactly sure if it's going to work or not, so they don't fully commit. In fact, after our first month, we barely moved the needle. In our second month, we faced similar results. Even I was starting to doubt our plan, my team reminded me that we had a plan we had to stick to. "Stick to the plan," they would tell me. That's when I knew we were going to make this work. After two months, they were committed to the plan even when my commitment waivered. When they were so involved in the plan that they had to tell me to stick to the plan, that was a great feeling.

They stuck to the plan and made sure everyone knew they were committed to the plan. Banners were everywhere, on every wall in their area (remember the section on the importance of reminders). Cards were printed and given to every employee. T-shirts were made. Emails were sent. PowerPoints were shared. Presentations were made. Everyone was hearing about the success, even though it was very slight at first, which only increased the excitement of the team. Improvements were obvious in the third month. Within a few short months, forward fuselage became a great place to work.

> Once people see a plan is working, that's when it's easy. Everyone wants to get on board at that point. The team is winning. Who doesn't want to be on a winning team? People wanted to know what

was going on. They were stopping and asking the mechanics how they were doing so well. People were smiling, John. They were smiling again.

The success—and strengthening of direction—continued. In fact, I heard about the success through one of their supervisors. In one of my leadership meetings, I heard someone from forward fuselage was in attendance. I approached her after the meeting. We talked for a bit, realizing we knew several of the same people. Then I asked her what made forward fuselage so successful. She didn't say the director. She didn't say an increase in resources or new equipment. Her response was two words and were provided without hesitation: "Hoshin Kanri."

"Really?"
"Yes. Hoshin Kanri."
"Okay. But was there anything else?"
"Well, yeah, but really it all comes down to Hoshin Kanri. Hands down."

After that, I was sold. Shortly after that, I was placed on a small team led by the director, where we were taught the principles of HK. I was fortunate to have the opportunity to be a part of an HK several more times and to facilitate many more even after I moved on from the company. Not all HKs work. It requires intense focus and trust from the whole group. When some groups realize the commitment required, they abandon efforts (remember the Pit of Despair?). The point is that HK, as do other strategic planning initiatives, get everyone together to sets goals, strategy and follow-up strategies on how the team is going to move forward. It is extremely powerful when an entire team commits to a plan.

Avoid Micro-managing

If I asked 20 people to make a paper airplane that could fly 20 feet, I would probably get 20 different types of paper airplanes, but I'm sure they would all fly 20 feet. Ideally, a good leader would be fascinated by the 20 different types of airplanes and choose a few prototypes that might be easily replicated for future business. A micro-manager would be involved in every step of the process and would ensure that all 20 planes used the same proven techniques to reach 20 feet. They'd most likely all look the same and most likely all fly the same, but they would all fly at least 20 feet. This sort of management can be a good thing, but often micro-managers believe theirs is the "right way." They tend to not be comfortable with a variety of ways.

Micro-managers know a really good way to make an airplane, so why not just follow their way to do it? Because micro-managers often decrease commitment in focus and direction as well as social trust. The micro-manager dismisses "bad" ideas immediately, while retaining the ones that most closely resemble the micro-manager's ideas. Thus, the airplane this team produces will look very similar to what the team produced the year before—and the year before.

Micro-managers tend to find intellectual difference less interesting and focus on getting the job done "the right way" (which is their way) the first time. The result is dependable, and it works. This isn't necessarily bad in all situations, but it can bad be when team members are fearful of taking risks or exploring options, knowing that the micro-manager will do whatever he/she would like to do. This causes a team to remain in a constant state of 5 in focus, direction and trust. The team members are capable people. The company hired them because they were capable people, but they need to constantly check with the manager to be sure they're not about to get in trouble.

This isn't an enjoyable way to work. Employees need the freedom to explore new ways and use their talents and abilities to excel. When employees believe they are able to make their own decisions, performance increases—as well as employee retention, extra-role behaviors, creativity, innovation and willingness to work longer hours.

There are many variables that can contribute to micro-management. Some are deep and may require professional help, but I've discovered that many micro-managers are displeased with the quality work of produced by their employees. For those wishing to avoid micro-managing employees, allow me to share something that was enlightening to me.

Situational leadership[5] is based on the relationship between the supervisor, the employee and the task. It is based on the answer to two questions: Does the employee know how to do the task, and how committed are they to completing the task? Here are the phases involved in situational leadership:

• When an employee is new to a task or at the lowest levels of commitment, a manager should act in a directive style of leadership. A directive style can be seen as handholding, checking in frequently, making sure progress is being made.
• From there, an employee progresses to being coached. In coaching, the manager is on the sidelines directing effort but allows the employee to carry out the work.
• The next phase is participative. Now the employee is much more independent, though the manager still checks in every once in a while to make sure things are moving forward.

- The final step is delegation. At this point, the employee is seen as fully functional, self-sustaining, capable of being in charge of the project and committed to the success.

The steps of situational leadership are only half of the theory. The other half is about how employees like to be treated.

If situational leadership is misapplied, it leads to a variety of negative consequences. If a person has zero experience accomplishing a task but the manager delegates projects to that person, the person is most likely to feel frustrated, set up for failure and distrusting toward the leader/organization.

The manager also is likely to feel frustrated because the manager just wants the job to be done. But instead, they're faced with constant direction seeking and guidance giving, diminishing time the manager would like to spend doing other tasks.

While this can be resolved with open communication and an investment of time, it's not a pleasant experience.

Now imagine this from the other side, the micro-managing side. Employee B enters the organization feeling fully capable of success. They are given a task that they feel they are competent enough to complete, but the manager swings by multiple times a day to check on progress. They continue to instruct on how to accomplish the task. Employee B is not hearing anything they don't already know, but they continue to be respectful—thinking the micro-managing will surely decrease with time.

It doesn't decrease with time. Imagine how employee B feels: unappreciated, undervalued and untrusted. Performance tends to decrease. Employee B will probably start considering a new job. If this only happened once, this problem could probably be resolved with employee B moving forward to fulfill a long career at the company. But if this is a constant trend, this will cause a problem, with very capable employees unable to reach their full potential.

Try New Things

A great way to build confidence in a new direction is to try new paths.

Wait! Doesn't this mean you could fail which means that you could lose people's commitment?

Well, maybe, but think about what you signal to employees when you try new things. Being open to experimenting new, unexplored paths signals that you're not giving up, that you are willing to commit resources to trying new paths that research shows could be beneficial to your organization. As American rock band Smash Mouth said in their world monster hit "All-star," "You never know if you don't go." If you're communicating to your employees that you need improvements, but you're not willing to try new things, I'm not sure your message is going to get across. Trying something new may help you find a new path to that new mountain top with greener grass and better pizza (as discussed in Chapter 8). You never know if you don't go.

Yes, you may fail. That happens quite a bit. New ideas are risky, but if an idea fails, instead of highlighting the failure, highlight what you learned.

Many organizations have suggestion boxes. Many employees have "open-door policies." Many say they're open to new ideas. Wouldn't that be excellent if you could actually show them that you're open to new ideas?

A Failed Plan Isn't Necessarily a Failure

Not every failure is a complete failure. There's tremendous learning that can happen in failure that can improve future possibilities. Many of the top companies today have a long list of failures that are then used in a different form in another product later. Remember, businesspeople don't fail. Rather, we reallocate our resources to more profitable ventures.

Listen to a story about a world-famous company that started off down a much different path. It's a great story of plan adjustment in order to survive. After reallocating their resources several times, they eventually their niche, developed their plan and became a major superpower but only after many failed attempts.

In 1889, a young man realized that there was a need for someone to print card games.[6] At this time in his town of Kyoto, many of the card games were handmade and included several variations. He saw a need and decided to fill it by opening up a card shop. His first product was *hanafuda*, a group of beautifully illustrated cards used for a variety of card games. He hired a group of artists to hand-make all of his cards, which were sold in shops around Kyoto and eventually to the surrounding areas.

By the 1930s, the company, now helmed by his grandson, had grown considerably, shipping cards throughout the surrounding countries. The onset of World War II slowed sales, but the company recovered quickly, as people affected by the war looked for an escape. In 1953, the company made a tremendous leap into the future by printing cards on durable plastic. Sales soared.

In 1956, the little card company had become a respectable player in the playing card industry. In an attempt to create additional opportunities for his company, the grandson flew to Cincinnati to see the operations of the largest playing card company in the world. The United

States Playing Card Company sold millions of card packs a year, but when the grandson saw the small, limited markets his product sold in, he realized that the playing card company was limited in size, scale and offerings. His company was destined to fail unless they found new ways and new markets. They were going to have to commit to a new plan.

The lack of potential the grandson noticed wasn't because of a lack of planning. On the contrary; this company had many great plans. Their board had a five-year plan that was developed through research in both current and future sales growths, but new information suggested that his company needed to be much more robust to survive the major conglomerates that they'd be competing against in the future. Their great plan shifted.

Their innovations started three years later in 1959, when the card company struck a deal with Disney to make playing cards with Disney characters. The deal delivered a tremendous break.

With the added revenue from the Disney cards, the company president decided to venture into a variety of businesses, none of which really panned out very well. Some were even considered failures and resulted in strategic adjustments. Then in 1964, with the growth and availability of electronic entertainment, Japan decided playing cards weren't as needed as they once were. The stock plummeted 80%, and the company barely scraped by the next two years. Again, failure was imminent unless they tried something new.

For the second time in a decade, the company was facing another major shift. The leader needed to change the plan for the company to survive because their current plan would not work. The world was changing too quickly.

They tried several attempts at various products, but none of them worked. This only fueled their determination to find a functional plan that would keep the company afloat.

Then in 1966, the company came out with a new toy called Ultra Hand, a mechanical arm inspired by one of the mechanical arms in the card printing factory. It was a blockbuster success that led to many more blockbusters.

Within a few years, the company was all-in within the electronics business. They had finally found a plan that worked—where they could thrive.

During this time, they were constantly finding "new peaks" to pursue, and they all seemed to work. The company began producing success after success.

They began producing electronics for arcade games and home consoles. The 1972, Magnavox Odyssey especially interested the toymaker. They thought home electronics were the future.

The company continued to work in the home entertainment industry until the console crash in 1983. After a meteoric growth with Atari and other home consoles, the market failed to control the quality and supply of the games, allowing games to be published without the consent of the console. This, compounded against recession in the 1980s and the introduction of home computers, caused a tremendous drop in console sales. The company had a system it was trying to publish with Atari called the Famicom (family computer), but Atari decided not to combine with the successful electronics company.

Again, the company faced a crisis in their direction. Their plan was interrupted with multiple environmental changes that caused a disruption to their plan. Now the company faced a problem. They needed a new plan and new commitment to their plan. The board proposed perhaps the riskiest plan of all, a plan that could bankrupt the company if it failed, but if it was successful . . . well, they could only imagine it would be, at that point. There were a lot of "ifs" to their plan, but the board and the employees were behind their strategy. They moved forward with implementing their new, innovative strategy.

After learning from previous console failures and putting safety measures in place for product quality, the company decided to roll out its new system in 1985. By 1986, nearly everyone knew someone with a Nintendo Entertainment System in their home.

Nintendo continued with several extremely successful ventures, exclusively publishing such hits as Super Mario Brothers and Zelda. Rivals appeared but couldn't compare to the extreme success of the behemoth Nintendo—until 1994, when Sony released its PlayStation.[7]

Nintendo continued to face challenges and strategic plan shifts. It changed the world with the introduction of the Wii, then became a laughingstock with the Wii U. Finally, it turned things around again with the Switch.[8]

The point of this story is failure was not necessarily because of poor planning or poor leadership. Each "failure" or plan shift led to Nintendo's next success. Failure is a part of learning. When change was needed, Nintendo wasn't afraid to try something new. It failed several times but stuck to it and eventually became the mega giant it is today.

Notes

1. Harter, J. (2021, August 18). Obsolete annual Reviews: Gallup's advice. Gallup.com. Retrieved from www.gallup.com/workplace/236567/obsolete-annual-reviews-gallup-advice.aspx
2. Ross, J. (2009, March). Lean/six sigma. It's a lifestyle. personal.
3. EKU. (2020, July 22). The seven wastes of lean manufacturing. EKU Online. Retrieved from https://safetymanagement.eku.edu/blog/the-seven-wastes-of-lean-manufacturing/

4. Ross, J. (2012, January). Hoshin Kanri Works! personal.
5. Blanchard, K. (2013). *Leadership and the one minute manager*. Harper & Row.
6. History of Nintendo, updated 2021. (2009, April). Nintendo Fandom. Retrieved from https://nintendo.fandom.com/wiki/History_of_Nintendo
7. Sirani, J. (2021, August 11). Where switch, ps4 rank among the best-selling video game consoles of all time. IGN. Retrieved from www.ign.com/articles/2019/10/30/top-15-best-selling-video-game-consoles-of-all-time
8. Clark, P. A. (2021, June 10). Thank Nintendo's failed Wii U for the switch's wild success. Mashable. Retrieved from https://mashable.com/2018/01/31/nintendo-switch-wii-u-failure-success/.

Chapter 15

Increasing Team Trust

Trust is the secret sauce of an extraordinary team. As previously discussed, a team can get the job done without trust, but the highest and most extraordinary teams have the highest levels of social trust.

To start off my suggestions for improvement, it is important to note the power of perceptions. Many times, group trust is at various levels simply because a few people perceived another few people to be different than they really are. They interpret actions in a way that confirms their belief. Perception is everyone's own reality. Thus, if person A believes person B is laughing at them, then person B laughed at them . . . according to person A. Managing these perceptions is difficult, but most can be overcome simply by people getting to know each other, building positive experiences together and realizing that each person is a powerful addition to the team, if they choose to be.

The suggestions presented next are some strategies to overcome perceptions, build trust and improve team unity.

The Power of Humor in Building Social Trust

Humor is a great connecting bond and tends to accompany psychological safety, the concept we explored in the chapter on the trust component, along with openness, increased sharing, and, of course, social trust.

Think of it like this. We all have emotional banks. We make deposits into this banks every day. Taking breaks, hanging out with friends, sleep, eating a healthy diet, relaxing on a beautiful day, all these things add to our emotional banks. Life demands withdrawals from our emotional banks. Our assignments at work, the responsibilities of our roles outside of work, all of these things make withdrawals from our emotional bank. When our banks reach into the negatives, we may have sudden fits of selfishness when we yell and eat ice cream because we just want to do what we want to do. If our bank is at zero long enough, then it may lead to burnout.

DOI: 10.4324/9781003269038-23

Humor provides a fantastic deposit into our emotional banks. It is a tremendous tool for buffering the effects of stress. It has also been shown to increase productivity in teams, increase the bond between leaders and subordinates, increase affective commitment to the workplace and even increase a person's overall physical and mental health. Why? Because humor bonds people together.[1] It is both a sign and a reinforcer of social trust.

Humor is a tremendous bonder. Humor has also been shown to increase cohesiveness, build strong bonds of friendship and increase strong bonds of connectedness even through race, gender, social status and workplace status differences. It is a belonging cue, signaling to the receiver of humor that she/he is accepted here.[2] Think about it. When two people are able to laugh at the same joke, it signals that the two have quite a bit in common. The sender is signaling to the receiver that he/she is open to talk. If the receiver reciprocates with more humor, then the bonds immediately strengthen.

Comedians depend on this bond between them and their audiences for a successful show. Jerry Seinfeld is one of the most successful comedians of all time, and we can learn something about social trust from his history and practices. His TV show, *Seinfeld*, ran for 10 seasons, won many awards and continues to earn hundreds of millions of dollars, as streaming sites bid for exclusive rights to stream. In 2011, Jerry started a show titled *Comedians in Cars Getting Coffee*. The premise is simple: Funny people drive in unique cars and go visit different coffee shops. They eat breakfast food, drink coffee and talk. That's it. And he also gets paid millions for it!

The most interesting part about the show are the discussions they have about their experiences as comedians. Comedians are interesting because they come off as calm, cool and collected, seamlessly guiding us through their prepared stories and punchlines. It seems, therefore, almost unbelievable that these comedians were ever nervous. On *Comedians*, during some of his discussions, we learn that some comedians used to vomit before shows. Others would pace with their nervous energy. Many smoked or drank before shows. Some even did so on stage while performing. While they all had their different ways of coping with pre-show stress, they all seem to agree that the ultimate cure for stress was *laughter*.

Decades of research confirms this. Laughter builds bonds, increases social trust and reduces stress.

As the comedians discuss with Jerry, when they would come out and tell their first joke on stage and receive what they felt was an adequate response, it would have a calming effect on their jitters. As their performance rolled on, if the laughter continued, the nerves started to dissipate, and the comedy show was often a great success.

Laughter is a sign that you're willing to play. You recognize the punchline delivered by the person as well-delivered, thus you reward them with a laugh.

Humor is incredibly powerful in building teams, which is why it can help social trust to grow so quickly. Even though two people may start at a level 1 in social trust, trust in the process. Use goodwill behaviors and humor as appropriate. Continue to build, let the other person reciprocate and by the end of the night, you may be at a 10.

Encourage Open Communication

Most people begin social situations guarded. They are unsure of what may happen and who may take advantage of their weaknesses, thus they create defensive barriers to reduce their chances of harm. While these barriers can protect them from mental and emotional harm, they also prevent teams from growing closer together.

There are several reasons to stay guarded in an organization. The workplace is a competition filled with rewards. Extrinsically, the workplace provides resources, status, projects, pay and promotions. Intrinsically, the workplace provides feelings of accomplishment, growth, autonomy, social interactions and accomplishment, but these rewards are not provided to everyone. One must compete for these resources. Sometimes the requirements are low, but these resources are not guaranteed in any job. Thus, some employees remain guarded, so they can stay focused on pursuing the rewards they seek or prevent themselves from losing the rewards they've already gained.

This is a form of survival, but teamwork needs interdependence in order to be the most effective. This requires open communication.

Nine Ways to Build Trust in Communications

For someone to know that you trust them, you need to send them the right messages.

Earlier we discussed communication. Communication refers to the messages we send in an engaged exchange.

Everything we do sends messages. We send messages even when we're not in an exchange. For example, when we meet someone new, we may act excited, give a warm handshake, touch their elbow, laugh at their jokes and provide every cue possible to help them to feel welcome and signal that they belong. That's all verbal and nonverbal communication.

The next day, what happens if we pass the new person in the hallway without acknowledging them? We then stand next to them in line in the cafeteria with barely a smile. Finally, the new person says something, and we act like we remember them, but then ask the person where we met. We communicated clearly yesterday that we care for this person and that they belonged, but then today, the message we unintentionally sent was that we were disinterested in them and that yesterday was just a show, just being polite. We didn't intend to send that message, but we're always sending messages. We cannot help it!

We constantly send messages to our team. Most of them are neutral messages, like what we eat for lunch or what we wear. When we use our messages effectively, we can tremendously impact our team.

We've already discussed a few message themes that are common on successful teams. I've put together a tactical list I've developed with the help of a few articles. Utilize as many as you can and be authentic! Your team members can sense inauthentic attempts.

1. Make Sure Everyone on the Team Talks and Listens in Roughly Equal Measure[3]

If someone isn't sharing, consider asking for their opinion on something. If someone is shy, you can give them a heads up that you'll be calling on them, saying something like, "Alex, after Bob shares, I'd like to hear your opinion on project X." This sends a great signal that you're interested in what they have to say.

2. Face the Person You Are Speaking With, Putting Down Distractions[4]

Use energetic gestures in your conversations. Put down your phone, look up from your computer and look people in the eye. What a great message to send, that the person you are speaking to is more important than anything else going on in your life. If you're in the middle of something and need to check your phone, let them know you're not ignoring them.

3. Spend Time With Your People[5]

You may only have one team, but that one team is made up of several individuals. Each individual needs to feel supported by the organization, team members and especially her/his leader. Find reasons to connect with each team member, not just the team leader in charge. Making these direct connections shows that you care and helps to build trust.

It can be work related or not but be sure to hold conversations even outside of formal meetings. If you see a team member in the hallway, greet them. The informal conversations are often how people bond the most. It shows you're not just using them to get work done but that you actually care about their well-being and about them as a person. People tend to respond well to feeling cared about.   .

4. Eat Lunch With People[6]

People love food, but sometimes we avoid lunch, which is weird because we love food. If you're looking for an excuse to build a relationship with a team member, buy them lunch. Research shows that those who make time for a lunch break are more productive at work and emotionally stronger. It's also another strong signal that the person belongs in the group. Encourage others to reap these benefits by taking them to lunch.

What if there's a person that you feel uncomfortable being one on one with? One if it's a person of another gender, you wouldn't want to cause rumors. If you feel uncomfortable meeting with them one on one in this manner, then invite a few people along or do it in a public place like the workplace cafeteria. Food is a great reason to bring people together, and it's difficult to turn down a free lunch.

5. Help Your Team Members[7]

This is one of the fastest ways to build trust.

Task performance is your work on a task. Contextual performance is your ability to build up those around you, to maintain the system in which task performance can thrive. Contextual performers are possibly more important than task performers because everyone benefits from a contextual performer. Task performance isn't everything. Contextual performance, or helping those around you to grow and improve, is an extremely powerful way to build trust among a team. It sends the signal that you care about their success in the workplace so much that you're willing to sacrifice your time to help them.

6. Get to Know the People Around You

Joe from the University of Washington rowing team felt more comfortable around the rowers when he felt he had more in common with them. This is absolutely true for most people. Get to know those around you. Open up to them but don't be a "me monster." The point is for you to get to know *them*. If they are really passionate about something, get to know it, too; then talk to them about it. People love knowing when someone listens to their recommendations. Learn to appreciate and even love the people around you.

One of my students was strongly into electronic dance music. He was an aspiring DJ, performing in local spots around the area. I asked him for some music recommendations. His initial response was, "What for?" When I told him I wanted to listen to it, he perked up. I told him I loved music, that it was a major part of my life. He gave me a list of people to listen to. I listened to them and provided feedback. He was over the moon! I even included some of the groups in my instruction. In our next meeting, he opened up about so much more than just music. It was excellent.

Care enough about your people to truly get to know them. Authentic relationships establish social trust.

7. Don't Be a "Box Checker"

Box checkers are the people who almost seem as if they're checking the boxes as they're talking, doing things out of obligation or suggestion rather than because they truly care.

One manager I worked with went around to her employees every day. She said hello and asked how they were doing each morning. She sometimes even made an additional comment or two. This seems great, right? This is exactly what many great leaders do with their teams . . . except she did not send caring messages. It was almost as if someone told her she needed to talk to her employees every day, so she made the rounds begrudgingly. Her voice was overly caring, like a preschool teacher talking to a student—but it wasn't authentic. She often cut off her employees while they were speaking to go over the daily to-do list. She even had a fake laugh that the employees would talk about and mock. Maybe she did care, but her stress about the to-do list of needing to talk to each employee every day was overwhelming her mind.

I get it. Maybe she really didn't like that part of her job, but isn't that exactly the problem? If you don't like working with your team, then ask yourself if you are in the right line of work. If you believe you are in the right line of work, then find reasons to like your team. It may not be easy, but it is definitely worth it.

Some have asked, "Yeah, but isn't box checking better than nothing?" My response, "Maybe." It might be good, or it might cause more harm than good. That doesn't mean don't do it. That means find a way to make it authentic.

8. Avoid Issuing or Expressing Social Judgement

I'm not saying you have to agree with everyone, but when someone feels judged, most clam up to protect themselves. That is exactly the opposite of what you want! You can disagree without eye rolling, smirking, laughing or making fun of someone, but as soon as you do, the person is far less likely to engage in an open conversation with you. I made that mistake in one of my classes.

It was with a student I previously enjoyed a great relationship with. We joked in class. She participated. It was a good student–professor relationship, until I screwed it up. I asked the class to raise their hand and tell me someone they cared about. It was going to be an object lesson about something. I don't remember what. Funny how well I remember the experience, but I don't even remember the point I was trying to make.

When you ask open-ended questions to a large class, you definitely need to be prepared for whatever may happen.

In this case, I was in an off mood, wasn't on my A game, when a student responded with a name. I asked what the relation was with this person she named.

She said it was her cat.

It caught me off guard. I love pets, and I love cats, but I wasn't expecting someone to say that person they cared about was a cat. I laughed. Then I said "Okay, what *person* do you care about?"

She replied, "My cat is a person to me."

Oof. I did not recover well. The relationship was different after that. She never came to my office again, and we never spoke. Regardless of your beliefs on cats, I laughed at something that was important to her, that she shared with me. I didn't validate her response. Instead, I made her feel like she was the weird one for caring for an animal as a person. I was in the wrong, and I didn't correct it well.

If you are fostering openness and building trusting relationships through communication, you can expect your team's trust—and therefore unity—to increase if you're sending signals that would diminish their values. Again, you don't have to agree with them but don't pass judgement.

I try to live by a quote by Ralph Waldo Emerson: "Shall I tell you the secret of the true scholar? It is this: Every man I meet is my master in some point, and in that I learn of him."

Every person you meet knows more than you on some topic. Try to find that topic or topics and learn from them. Most people really enjoy sharing what they're passionate about. Try asking a professor what their key research areas are and what their favorite research projects are. They'll *love* having someone who actually wants to hear all the nerdy details about their research. This isn't unique to professors; it's a people thing. We worked hard to learn about what we know. It's fun to share.

People are awesome. Find a way to learn from everyone. It's great for social trust.

Notes

1. Mesmer-Magnus, J., Glew, D., & Viswesvaran, C. (2012). A meta-analysis of positive humor in the workplace. *Journal of Managerial Psychology, 27,* 155–190. 10.1108/02683941211199554.

2. Romero, E. J., & Cruthirds, K. W. (2006). The use of humor in the workplace. *Academy of Management Perspectives*, 20(2), 58–69.
3. Pentland, A. S., Woolley, A., & Malone, T. W. (2015, July 15). The new science of building great teams. *Harvard Business Review*. https://hbr.org/2012/04/the-new-science-of-building-great-teams
4. Pentland, A. S., Woolley, A., & Malone, T. W. (2015, July 15). The new science of building great teams. *Harvard Business Review*. https://hbr.org/2012/04/the-new-science-of-building-great-teams
5. O'Hara, C. (2020, January 10). How to work with someone who isn't a team player. *Harvard Business Review*. Retrieved September 29, 2021, from https://hbr.org/2017/04/how-to-work-with-someone-who-isnt-a-team-player
6. Tulshyan, R. (2021, January 21). Take your lunch break! *Harvard Business Review*. Retrieved from https://hbr.org/2021/01/take-your-lunch-break
7. Motowildo, S. J., Borman, W. C., & Schmit, M. J. (1997). A theory of individual differences in task and contextual performance. *Human Performance*, 10(2), 71–83.

Chapter 16

Decreasing Team Conflict

Relational conflict is interesting because it can be difficult to give advice on what to do when two people don't like each other. As a parent, you might say, "Just stay away from them," knowing that in a kid's world, things have a working themselves out. Unfortunately, it's not that simple as adults.

To provide a real solution, you'd need to be able to talk to each person and see what is going on—why the conflict exists—and create a solution together. You may have guessed it by now, but this book does not come with a counseling session for me, you and one other to resolve a conflict. Even if it did, I'm not sure you'd want me negotiating a resolution for your conflict. I'm pretty good, but I'm sure there are others that may be in a better situation. However, the good news is that not only can conflict resolution skills be taught, and as previously mentioned, 95% of all of people that receive conflict resolution training have improved in some way.

The following is a list of strategies and tactics you might want to use to buffer the negativity that often accompanies a conflict resolution. Some of these suggestions are actually related to handling tough situations with employees. I included these with relational conflict because if a situation is handled poorly, then it can definitely and very quickly lead to relational conflict. And as we all know, thanks to all of the survival shows on all the streaming sites, the best way to survive is to never get in a situation where survival is needed!

The #1 way to reduce conflict is to prevent it. Do what you can to prevent the conflict from starting by practicing good communication techniques and building high levels of social trust.

Some may have read this and thought, "Saweet! Justification for avoiding conflict." Nope. Not at all what I'm saying. Employ excellent strategies to avoid relational conflict among your team and between your team members, but if conflict does arise, address it.

DOI: 10.4324/9781003269038-24

Stay Calm

Whether you're the one having the relational conflict or you're the one just trying to help resolve the conflict, there's a chance the ire will be directed at you. Stay calm. Remember that we have all said things that we don't mean and that relational conflict is the culinary kitchen of chaos baking up all sorts of regretful sayings and actions. Keep a calm tone. Breathe. If things stay intense, then take a five-minute break and approach the situation later—but stay calm throughout. It's very difficult to be angry with someone who is not angry back.

Focus on the Behavior

Relational conflict, as explained earlier, is when people just don't seem to get along. On a deeper level, it exists because one person exhibits behaviors that are disagreeable with another person's demeanor or behavior. Values are often compromised as well. That's a mouthful, so I simplified it earlier. Really, though, it's about *behaviors*. Someone did something that is not appreciated by someone else. That *behavior* needs to be addressed, not the *person*. Here are some tactics to keep your communication focused on the behavior:

- Avoid "you" statements: "Well, when you did this. . . ." That's attacking the person. Try something like this instead: "When _____ happened, it frustrated me because. . . ." It may sound cheesy, but it works.
- Listen to what they're saying but bring it back to their behavior—something you can observe someone doing. Instead of saying someone has a "bad attitude," for example, describe what you can see. Did the person roll their eyes in a meeting? Share that observation.
- Careful not to get sidetracked—when someone's behavior is being addressed, the accused will often point to someone else or some other reason that he/she believes their poor choice was adequate for the situation. There may be some truth to their statement but focus on the behavior of the person you are speaking to, assuring them you'll look into the situations they brought up but that their reaction to the situation was not appropriate. As they share their "reasons" for the behavior, don't be afraid to repeat your main point if you find yourself feeling derailed in the conversation. Listen, consider their input but don't cave on addressing the behavior.

Timing Can Make a Big Difference

By now, you've read my countless warnings about the danger of relational conflict. I've also made several recommendations to get rid of it quickly. Even though relational conflict is so detrimental to the organization, handling it at the wrong time heaps fuel on the fire.

It's hard to say when the right moment is because some conflict should be addressed immediately, whereas some may be better one on one at another time. A lot of it depends on the relationship you have with the employee. I can say that it's rarely the right time when you're in front of everyone. Conflict can grow more conflict. Trying to solve a conflict in front of a group of people can cause more conflict to happen and it definitely can hurt the relationship between you and the people involved in conflict.

Again, sometimes this is necessary, but if possible, address the conflict with the person one-on-one, away from onlookers. This is a good practice for many reasons, but one of the big ones is because we all have our reputations to think about. Being talked down to by the boss in front of others hurts way more than if the boss had spoken to you in private. When we're in front of people, our defenses are up. We tend to let our defenses down a little when we're one on one.

The conflict may even need to be handled a few days later, especially when in the midst of creative endeavors. I recently interviewed a member of a big-time improvisational comedy troupe, The Thrillionaires, for my upcoming book. They had just completed their third season of their show *Show Offs*. The topic of our discussion was on teamwork in unique workplaces. Conflict management was part of it. Here are two pieces of advice from Lisa Valentine Clark:

- Correcting in the moment can decrease creativity and performance. Plus, many people are self-aware and evaluate their own performance. Give them a chance to evaluate their own performance first. Wait until the next rehearsal and discuss it there.
- Correct patterns. Everyone has a bad day or a brain misfire because they're distracted. Correcting someone on every little thing is micromanaging and not necessary with professionals. If something happens, watch it. If there's a pattern, address it.

Again, some things are so important that they need to be addressed almost immediately. Safety issues are definitely like that. I'll share a brief situation of my own experience in this area. I will never forget my first day leading a union manufacturing team. All I did was share an announcement from upper management. Somehow that led to an explosion of anger, all directed at me. There were very direct comments. The resistance was led by two ringleaders. These two ringleaders got the entire crew fired up. Trying to handle the situation in that moment would have been fruitless. It was 30+ to one. It wouldn't have gone over well, and I had zero social capital with the group. I ended the meeting, absolutely unsure what I was going to do, but I knew something had to be done. I had the inspiration to get to know them.

About two hours later, I called the first ringleader to my desk. We just chit chatted for ten minutes, building a foundation, finding a common ground. I then explained that what happened in the meeting couldn't happen like that again. To my surprise, he apologized! I told him I appreciated him and that I needed his help with this team. We shook hands. He left.

Ringleader two came in. Same result. Turns out these were two people who truly cared about their jobs and were passionate about success. They were tired of feeling like management was against them. The meetings not only reduced conflict, but they also provided useful information for me as I moved forward with my team.

Passion takes many forms. Conflict is one of them.

We shook hands. The three of us never had a conflict with each other again. Not bad for a first day! (I've never told them this, but I was so nervous! It ended well, though.)

Pick a good strategic time, away from onlookers to resolve relational conflict.

Build a Relationship of Trust

Of all the conflict resolution books and articles I've read and the studies I've been a part of, rarely do I hear about the importance of a relationship in resolving conflict. This surprises me because in my experience, a relationship goes a long way. It's part of social trust.

When you have a relationship with someone, you have built social trust. When social trust is high, you can correct people more easily because they trust that you aren't trying to hurt them.

It's similar when solving relational conflict. If you have many great experiences with a person, then solving relational conflict is a lot easier.

A sidenote about conflict: Sometimes people are so stressed about the need to resolve conflict correctly that they avoid conflict all together. Here's a secret that many authors of conflict books don't want you to know: There's no single, surefire way to handle conflict. Yeah, there's no way that will always be right or successful. There are some wrong ways, but in general, as long as it comes from the heart and from a position of truly wanting to salvage the relationship, then as rough as it can be in the moment, it can be resolved. The reason why is because you've already built up a relationship of trust, so even if you do "mess it up," they'll be far more likely to forgive you.

Trust can actually be built while handling conflict. Here's a tip when handling conflict. This comes from a study I found done with several hundred eighth graders. For the purpose of this study, the eighth graders wrote papers, and the teachers were asking them to rewrite their papers with the corrections. They tried different methods, but the one that stood out by far as the most effective used these key points in this order:

- You're a valuable member of this team.
- We hold our team to a higher standard. Your behavior isn't up to par.
- We want you to stay on our team. We want to help you improve your behavior.

You can adjust the wording to fit your team best, but essentially, when you tell an employee that you value them and want them to be a part of your team but that they're going to have to step it up (being behaviorally specific about what that means), they tend to step it up.

Students who believed they could be part of the team wrote more than 50% more than those who used other methods to get them to correct their papers, a dramatic increase, especially for eighth graders.

Since reading that study, a colleague of mine and I introduced it to a manufacturing company we were working with. They loved it and found an improvement in results as well. I've used it on my kids. Its tough work to be a part of the Ross family (ha, not really).

It really does work. Give it a try.

After Conflict Resolution, Increase Your Caring Actions

This goes along with messaging. I know very few people who actually enjoy handling conflict. Most don't like it, and many avoid it. Conflict resolution normally isn't fun for anyone involved, even if you're not at the center of the conflict. Emotions are high. Defense mechanisms are high. Reputations are needing to be salvaged. There's an excuse for everything. Ugh. It's not fun.

Imagine this: You are the boss. You have two employees causing trouble. You work it out with them. Then, the next day, you avoid them for fear it might be awkward. What are the two employees thinking about you? How do you think those two employees perceive your attitude toward them? Or, worse yet, what if you talk to one of them and avoid the other? What message is that sending?

I can tell you what they are most likely feeling because I've looked into this. They're thinking you don't like them. You're disappointed in them, and now you're ignoring them.

Guess what that does to employee performance? That's right. When we feel like our bosses have put us in the "out group," we do not tend to work as hard. We tend to look for other jobs. We feel lonely. Backbiting and gossiping increase, as a way to cope with the "injustice" that's occurring. You could lose a great employee because the conflict resolution was not followed up with an increase in caring.

After a resolution, people are probably feeling hurt and embarrassed. Make sure to continue to invite them to events—and ask for their contribution. Joke with them. Give them another project. Make a point not to avoid them. If you only have time to visit half of your employees, make sure to visit the employees you recently had a resolution with. Repairing the relationship quickly will show them that you are ready to move on if they are. It will also help show that it's not them that you don't like; it's their behavior. You still like them and want them to stay, but you just want that behavior to change.

Again: Repair the relationship quickly. Show an increase in caring.

Now that you've explored how to decrease relational conflict—the fourth component of The Unity Formula—it's time to explore some fun details and facts about how it all fits together!

Chapter 17

Fun Facts About The Unity Formula

As I shared, I've used The Unity Formula with teams across the country in six different industries. After using the formula many, many times, I discovered that there are some interesting trends when using the formula. Here are some of my findings using The Unity Formula.

The Unity Formula Scores Indicate Five Major Divisions

Teams using this formula tend to fall in one of five categories. The categories are briefly described below:

1. **1%–19%**—Low-performing teams (as determined by team members and management). These poor teams are missing out on 80%+ of their potential! These teams are often riddled with problems and conflict. At the beginning of the book, I asked you to think about your best team ever, then your worst team ever. Your worst team ever probably fit into this category.
2. **20%–40%**—Average teams. Remember mean, median and mode? Well, this is the mode. Most teams fall in this category. I've had one person mention that this didn't make sense to her. Wouldn't average be 50%? Well, no. Would you watch a movie that was 50% on Rotten Tomatoes or visit a restaurant that was 2.5 stars on Google or Yelp? Probably not. We have standards. We don't necessarily want a restaurant or movie that falls in the middle. The middle is not necessarily average. In this case, most teams in the workplace are working to get by. They're not trying to excel or anything, just putting in a day's work.
3. **41%–70%**—High-performing teams. This is a broad range, but teams in this category share similar traits and performance. Great teams to be a part of. As previously stated in the earlier chapters,

DOI: 10.4324/9781003269038-25

even if your team never makes it to an extraordinary team (ET) but *does* make it to this level, you should consider that a victory! More work to be done, but this is a great team. This is about the level that relational conflict is almost nonexistent. That's how damaging relational conflict is to a team. The existence of it will make it extremely difficult to move beyond an average team. These teams are often what people think of when they think of their favorite teams. Many people have yet to be a part of an ET. They enjoyed being on their high-performing team. They love it when I tell them their team can be even better. Hopefully this book will help more ETs exist.

4. 71%–89%—Teams are always fluctuating. We are humans and are constantly battling distractions. Teams at this level are extremely similar to ETs and are either on their way up to an ET or may have even been an ET earlier but are just having a rough day/moment. A few slight adjustments and increases in unity, and this team is an ET.
5. 90%–100%—ET

Executive Teams Are Often the Least Unified of Them All!

I wasn't expecting this. I respected executives and wanted to be like them. I was expecting to find executive teams to be the most unified. After all, most do not reach this level through luck. They have to work for it, be an achiever and make things happen. They almost all have experiences being on great teams, but when it comes to working together as executives, they are generally terrible at it.

I was implementing The Unity Formula with an executive team at a multi-billion-dollar manufacturing company. I had discussed performance and teamwork with each of the vice (VPs) presidents and applied the formula with each of them. I asked them about their executive team, and their divisions and teams that they lead. They all thought that they led fairly unified teams, but they all thought their executive teams were terrible. The unity rating for their executive team was 1%–3%! I have rarely ever worked with teams that low. The VPs were in a heated competition to be the next chief operating officer (COO). The current COO at the time was young, ambitious and good at her job, but they were already positioning themselves as the obvious replacement. It was bad, but the evidence was clear:

*   They refused to save the company money if it meant that they'd have to go along with another VP's idea because it would mean that the other VP would look better.

- They would gossip like crazy, trying to create allies to make their division the most powerful.
- They openly mocked each other, definitely didn't trust each other, and while they understood the goal, they were not in agreement with how to accomplish the goal.
- They wanted their idea to be the one that caused them to meet the goal, not someone else's. It was an extremely selfish team climate.

In a meeting with the COO, I discussed with her how divided her executive team was. The comment didn't surprise her. She explained matter of factly that the next promotion for VPs in that company was to become a corporate (C) level leader. Becoming a C-level leader means your salary more than doubles and you get more stock, access to the company jet and your own private bathroom. She mentioned that just to get to their current level as VPs, they have to be competitive with other VPs. They're one promotion away from adding a C-level job to their resumes at a major company, which would absolutely increase their opportunities outside of the company should they choose to pursue them, and they were competing against other vice presidents who are also major competitors. Then she said, "They're all vying for my job. What they don't understand is that the person who gets my job isn't going to be a major competitor. It's going to be the person who can unify the group." She knew the value of unifying a team.

This was the lowest scoring executive team I worked with using The Unity Formula, but this is similar to other executive teams I've worked with without the formula. In fact, when I mention that executive teams tend to be the least unified teams to other executives, they tend to all react the same way. "Yeah, I can see that."

Generally, Most Teams Tend to Be Lower to Midlevel

This makes sense. On a normal day under normal circumstances, teams do not tend to be 100% unified. They're just getting by. They tend to be average. This is okay, though it could be better. They could benefit from increasing their focus, direction and trust while minimizing conflict.

The Most Commonly Unified Teams Tend to Be Emergency Response Teams—Such as in Hospitals

I alluded to this earlier: Emergency teams are excellent examples of how "normal" employees can become an ET when their focus, direction and trust align. An emergency tends to unify people very quickly. I have found that teams trained in emergency responses tend to be low to average on the unity scale during average times, non-emergency times, but when there's an emergency, they are at 100%. In an emergency situation, they are all fully committed to the goal and the plan. They trust each other, and relational conflict is out the window. They are working together to solve a major and potentially life-threatening problem. When the problem is over, they go back to picking on each other and causing problems. Emergency teams are very capable high-performing teams that are often only asked to be high performing under certain circumstances. When they're not in these situations for a long time, they get bored. Team leaders need to work to overcome that.

Sports Teams Are Difficult to Unify, But Once They Are, They Tend to Sustain Unity Well

Athletes have many competing priorities, especially today with social media and the recent name, image, likeness sponsorship rules for college athletes. They have to keep their social lives up while also maintaining their own physical abilities. Athletes tend not to put up with those giving less effort than themselves. They are competitive people who have put in many hours into reaching their peak level of performance. When they see other players not putting in the effort, they grow frustrated because their lack of effort hurts the whole team. When several members of the team (possibly 25%) aren't putting in the work required to excel, high athletic achievers tend to work independently—working as a team when necessary but otherwise keeping to themselves.

In my opinion, based on what I've seen and read, the main job of a coach is to keep the team unified. Of course, they need to teach and manage plays, develop their team's skills, etc. But if the team isn't unified, then the team won't realize its full potential. If they do reach a point of unification, however, they tend to feed off of each other's competitive spirit and tend to stay unified unless acted upon by an outside force.

Side note: Competitive people in the workplace tend to feel the same way as athletes about loafers. It's frustrating to see people who aren't trying because it brings the whole group down. This goes along with the rule of 25% I presented earlier. Sometimes the perceived social loafers actually are trying, but it might not be to the same standard or level that a competitive person might expect it to be. Our perception is our reality. A competitive person perceiving another to be a loafer is correct. A person who believes they are sincerely trying is also correct. They're both correct in their own minds. The expectations of the team need to be clear. This is also where social trust comes in. We have to trust that each of us is trying to be the best we can be, so we can excel as a team and that if anyone is falling below team expectations, then that person is notified, and performance is improved.

People Are Far Less Likely to Be on an Extraordinary Team If They Aren't Committed to the Organization

Groups with members who are not fully committed to the organization tend to be more difficult to unify. There could be many reasons for this. They may have felt slighted by the organization at some point, or they aren't in agreement with the organization. In these cases, instead of looking out for the benefit of the organization, they tend to look out for themselves. Whatever the cause may be, when employees are committed to the organization, they are more likely to provide extra work and extra hours. Perhaps what is even more powerful, though, is that they are more likely to provide the organization with more ideas, and they are more likely to commit to developing these ideas.

This highlights the important role of the organization in creating ETs. Hire people who are likely to have high levels of focus and direction, people who are likely to agree with the goals and strategy. Take care of your employees. This doesn't mean they have to be showered with money and benefits. If that were true, then few people would work for small businesses. Small business employees love that their ideas can make a difference. They love the small team, the family-like atmosphere. They stay because they love where they work, despite the often lower pay and fewer benefits than larger organizations can provide.

Once You Experience an Extraordinary Team, You Will Experience Frustration and Disappointment With Future Teams

The unfortunate consequence of being on an ET is that teams that aren't quite as unified are really frustrating. Once you've been on an ET, you know what potential a team has. You know that a team can be a great place to be, a place that can accomplish great things and be a tremendous part of your life with lots of great memories. It is frustrating to be on teams that don't realize this or to work with people that are refusing to devote the time or energy to the team.

Those that have experienced extraordinary success on an ET often form their own informal teams to pursue company strategies. They're still committed to the goals and strategies of the organization, but they may not agree with the teams they have to work with, so they sometimes go around it by forming informal groups.

Conclusion

We've covered a lot in this book. We started off talking about how unity is the single most important factor in team success and how through unity, just about every team problem can be addressed. We talked about the importance of believing that there are no good or bad teams, just teams on a scale—and how because they're on a scale, they can slide to more or less unified throughout their time together.

We then discussed the four key components to unity by maximizing focus, direction and trust and minimizing conflict. We then introduced the scale for each component. Then, The Unity Formula was introduced and practiced. Finally, several suggestions for improvement were presented—and we covered some fun facts and FAQs. That's a lot to cover!

I always like to point my students in the direction of further knowledge so that they can continue the learning process. There's so much more information out there on how to unify a team, though they may not explicitly state that their purpose is to build unity. I am a big fan of *11 Rings* by Phil Jackson, *The Culture Code* by Daniel Coyle and *The Trust Factor* by Paul Zak. These are three great books to supplement the learning in this book as well as the numerous other articles that can be found in the endnotes throughout.

Also, stay in touch. I love what I do, and love to share it with others. Maybe one day, we'll meet at a presentation at one of your companies or at a conference. If we're ever in the same place, please introduce yourself. I'd love to hear your thoughts about how you've increased unity in your workplace.

Finally, remember, there are various forms of art. Really, when we're admiring a sculpture, a painting or a musical performance, what we're really admiring is the person's amazing ability to use their talents. Well, to me, a well-run business is an art that can be just as powerful as any performing arts group. Well run businesses require hard work, practice and dedication. Many of the suggestions in this book take years

DOI: 10.4324/9781003269038-26

to expertly use, but you'll never get there if you don't practice. Start practicing. You'll see results and they'll be more frequent the more you practice. When you encounter an extraordinary team, respect them for the artwork that they are. My hope now is that you'll go forth and increase unity in all of your organizations, no matter how big or small. Go be artists.

Index

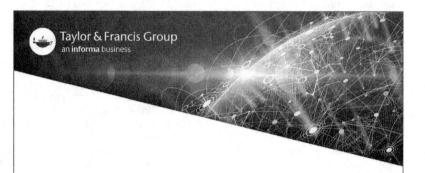

Printed in the United States
by Baker & Taylor Publisher Services